*Understanding Biblical Research*

LUIS ALONSO SCHÖKEL, S.J.

# *Understanding Biblical Research*

*Translated by*
*Peter J. McCord, S.J.*

HERDER AND HERDER

1963

HERDER AND HERDER NEW YORK

232 Madison Avenue New York 16, N.Y.

EL HOMBRE DE HOY ANTE LA BIBLIA was originally published
in Barcelona by Juan Flors.


Imprimi potest: Rev. Timothy A. Curtin, S.J.
Vice-Praepositus Prov. Neo-Eboracensis
October 24, 1962

Nihil Obstat: John R. Ready, Censor Librorum
January 6, 1963

Imprimatur: †Robert F. Joyce
Bishop of Burlington
January 7, 1963

Library of Congress Catalog Card Number: 63-11308
© 1963 Herder and Herder, Inc.
Printed in the United States of America

# Foreword

It is a matter of common knowledge that there has been a new "flowering" in Catholic scripture studies in recent times, dating roughly from the appearance of the encyclical of Pope Pius XII in 1943 on the promotion of biblical studies, *Divino afflante Spiritu*. This new "flowering" has been in many ways responsible for the general upsurge in interest in the Bible among Catholics of the last decade or so—an upsurge which no one can regret. The development has also been watched with favor and genuine satisfaction by many Protestant and Oriental Church theologians, with the result that many realize on all sides that it has been a vital contribution to the realistic, concrete convergence in today's ecumenical movement. It is, however, unfortunately not a matter of equally common knowledge that this recent "flowering" in Catholic scripture studies is the term of a process of maturation which has been at work for a long time. The maturing process is not easily described. And yet, some attempt to describe it is quite necessary today, in order to explain to modern Catholics and Protestants how this development has taken place in what appears to be such a short time. It is even less well known, and in fact more difficult to explain, *how* or *why* this thing *could* have happened. For the new

development seems to have ramifications and consequences in various areas of Catholic faith and dogma,
which many find difficult to explain or to account for.

Many are the questions which the new development
has raised and many are the aspects of that maturing
process which could be discussed. A number of Catholic writers in recent times have addressed themselves to
one or other of them. Among them is the author of this
book, Fr. Luis Alonso Schökel, a Spanish Jesuit, who is
professor of Old Testament exegesis and biblical theology at the Pontifical Biblical Institute in Rome. The
book will be welcomed in English dress especially by
those priests and sisters who took part in the Summer
Biblical Institutes held in the Chicago area during the
first two weeks in July, 1962, when Fr. Alonso Shökel
lectured so captivatingly on biblical inspiration and the
nature of biblical literature. His interest in literature
and his ability as a literary critic and exegete then became known to a fortunate group of American Catholics interested in the Bible. His approach to the Old
Testament is at once sound and refreshing; it is based,
not on a priori assumptions of what the Bible should
be saying, but on a personal confrontation with exegetical problems posed by the biblical books themselves.
His handling of these problems makes him a Spanish
exegete and biblical scholar of rare quality today.

But Fr. Alonso Schökel's name has become known to
modern readers through a recent attack on the Pontifi-

cal Biblical Institute in Rome. It was occasioned by an article published by him in the summer of 1960, "Dove va l'esegesi cattolica?" (*Civiltà cattolica*, 111 [September 3, 1960], 449–460), "Where is Catholic Exegesis Headed?" In it he tried to sketch the "new direction" in biblical studies since the encyclical of Pius XII. It was a brief effort of popularization which sought to explain to educated Italian readers the new Scripture development in a form slightly different from this book. There is no need to say more about that unfortunate episode here (cf. *Theological Studies*, 22 [1961], 426–444). Today the author continues to write and lecture on these subjects with his usual enthusiasm and competence.

In this book Fr. Alonso Schökel gives us the substance of three lectures which he delivered to Spanish university circles in San Sebastian and Madrid a few years ago. They were published at first in Spanish and subsequently translated into German (with some modifications). The favorable reviews of the Spanish original and of the German translation by persons of such competence as M.-E. Boismard, O.P., of the École biblique in Jerusalem, M. Zerwick, S.J., of the Pontifical Biblical Institute in Rome, J. P. Weisengoff, formerly of the Catholic University of America, make it obvious that this book has merits that deserve attention in the English-speaking world as well. To these voices we are happy to add our own recommendation.

It should be obvious that no single book is going to answer all the questions which have been raised by the new "flowering" in Catholic scripture studies. However, the perspective adopted by the author is one which is badly needed in this problematical area, viz., a historical one. For even if one cannot yet give a fully satisfying answer to the question *how* or *why* this development *could* have come about, it is usually important in such a matter to realize at least *how* the situation in fact developed. In surveying the biblical field from the sixteenth century on to the present, Fr. Alonso Schökel addresses himself to those modern Catholics, both clerical and lay, whose interest in the Bible has led them to ask about the recent development in scripture studies.

It is unfortunately common enough to meet an attitude of skepticism toward the modern biblical movement, an attitude which has been born of an exaggerated fear that it might "upset the apple cart." In looking back over the past half century, one can see that this attitude has been engendered within the Church by the reaction to the Rationalism and Modernism of the last century. That reaction was epitomized in the decrees of the Biblical Commission which were disciplinary directives on various controverted issues. At the time of their issuance they were needed; but they had the unfortunate effect of casting a dark cloud over much of Catholic biblical scholarship at the beginning of this century. That a change has taken place can be seen from the fact that there have been no similar decrees in recent times (aside from cautions issued in 1933 and 1953); even the most recent *monitum* on Scripture (dated June 20, 1961; see *Acta apostolicae Sedis*, 53 [1961], 507) was issued not by the Biblical Commission, but by the Holy Office. But it is understandable that scripture professors who were themselves trained under the dark cloud of reaction would pass on to their clerical students a conservative attitude, and that these in turn as pastors would inculcate the same in the laity. It is not difficult to explain, therefore, the existence of a skeptical attitude toward the modern biblical movement. But it is one that is not necessarily to be cherished. We feel that this book of Fr. Alonso Schökel will dispel some of that attitude by a sincere and frank discussion of many of the issues of the biblical problem of today.

Joseph A. Fitzmyer, s.j.
Woodstock College

# Translator's Preface

This book was originally published in Spanish under the title *El Hombre de hoy ante la Biblia* (Barcelona: Juan Flors, 1959). It was subsequently translated into German by Rudolf Reinhard and entitled *Probleme der biblischen Forschung in Vergangenheit und Gegenwart* (Düsseldorf: Patmos, 1961). In the German version the translator omitted several passages from the Spanish original and added a few paragraphs and footnotes of his own to make the book more suitable for his German readers.

The present version is based, for the most part, on the Spanish edition. For the same reason as the German translator, I have also omitted a few paragraphs. In addition, there are several passages which the author wanted to include in the English version, because he felt that they would shed greater light on some of the issues raised in the book. Lastly, I have added a number of footnotes which seemed to be required for the English translation. As a result of these changes, the present version supercedes to a certain extent both the Spanish original and the German translation. Further, this entire English version was corrected and approved by Fr. Alonso Schökel.

I would like to thank the many generous persons who

aided me in preparing this translation. Special thanks are due to Fr. Joseph A. Fitzmyer, S.J., whose suggestions and criticisms were invaluable.

PETER J. McCORD, S.J.

Woodstock College

# Contents

*Understanding Biblical Research*

# Chapter I.
# Difficulties
# and Their Conquest

The contemporary biblical scholar often runs into a thorny situation. It could be summarized as follows:

1) the public asks questions
2) the scholar gives answers
3) the public is scandalized

If we examine each point in this outline, we shall discover a number of significant facts. First of all, the public, comprised of professional men, intellectuals, and students, is asking questions because its curiosity has been aroused. Since we have long been aware of the Old Testament's existence, one might well ask why there is such a strong current interest in it. For the word, "Testament," till now has signified little more to us than some kind of a luminous cloud which indicates the divine presence, and demands a reverent response. The adjective, "Old," likewise, has suggested to us only vague glimmerings of the distant past. As for the contents of the book, it has produced neither interest nor motivation for the majority of the public. But all of a sudden the book began to stimulate people's curiosity, sow doubts in their minds, challenge them with difficult problems and force them to ask questions.

We must now attempt to account for this sudden change of attitude.

Let us look first at a somewhat analogous situation. For many years scientists had been studying the structure and splitting of the atom without producing any notable disturbance in the mind of the general public. When students learned the theories proposed by Niels Bohr, Ernest Rutherford and Max Planck, they had no further motive than that of passing their exams. But once the atomic bomb exploded over Hiroshima, its reverberations shook the whole world. The bomb immediately set up a "chain-reaction" of questions; for everyone wanted to know how the atom was split.

The present renewal of interest in the Bible did not occur as abruptly as the interest in atomic theory. Several important discoveries were made, of course, but they were greeted with exaggerated enthusiasm only because of the special circumstances in which they took place. For the most part, however, there has been a gradual and quiet development among biblical scholars, undisturbed by any serious controversies. Nevertheless a biblical movement *has* come into being and is certainly one of the more spectacular developments of the postwar period. Once this movement was created by enthusiastic Bible readers, ecclesiastical authority sanctioned and encouraged it. The movement has gathered ever-greater force through the continually increasing production of books on the Bible, biblical periodicals, and new translations of the Bible.[1] Some future historian will no doubt point to the biblical movement as a characteristic feature of mid-twentieth-century Catholicism. In fact, interest in the Bible has spread among Catholics to an extraordinary degree. And since the object of this interest is rather complex, the public is asking questions.

The fact, therefore, that the biblical scholar would attempt to answer the public should not seem at all unusual. It is only natural, after all, for a priest to solve a moral question for one of his parishioners. If the question is difficult and he is unable to answer it, he consults a moral theologian or looks the answer up in some technical book on the subject.

The case is similar with regard to questions concerning the Bible. The priest must either attempt to answer doubts about the Bible or else consult a biblical scholar for the answers. At this point we cannot tell whether the need for giving answers to the public will produce more biblical scholars or more moral theologians. What *is* clear is their distinct point of departure.

The difference lies in what has given rise to the questions. Life itself, not to mention art, often creates moral problems. It does this without any outside help, effortlessly, spontaneously. Modern biblical problems, on the other hand, have to a large extent been deliberately created by the specialists and scholars. This is actually what has chiefly created the biblical movement, namely those scholars who, with the best of intentions, have gone about scattering thistles in the comfortable beds of quiet and inertia. By cultivating the thorns of doubt, they have instituted a movement which comes as the response to a definite challenge. Now that the movement exists, it is sometimes difficult to say in the case of a specific problem whether it has arisen spontaneously or has been deliberately proposed; just as it is impossible to say *who* proposed it. Questions regarding the biblical account of our first parents (the serpent, the tree, Adam's rib, the apple) are obvious examples of problems the scholars themselves have created. But a real, and long-standing, question, such as the one about Jonah's sojourn in the whale's belly, can still be quite spontaneous.

The biblical scholars have at least carried out their activity in all sincerity. Their purpose has never been to upset the public, but rather to satisfy doubts or to limit them to a definite area. Their intentions are not sinister; they merely wish to jar the public at times from a dangerous complacency. In general, they are merely seeking to give honest answers to real problems. The answers will of course differ, since many problems have not reached any definite solution or even a commonly accepted explanation. In any case the scholars give the best answer they know of or at least offer their considered opinion.

A Catholic commentator of the seventeenth century could placidly tabulate the figures given in the biblical genealogies, add up the numbers arithmetically, and arrive at the conclusion that the Israelites entered Palestine in the year 2494 after the creation of the world. Such was the opinion of Cornelius a Lapide, who died in 1637. No modern commentator would dream of using biblical numbers so ingenuously. The results of recent archaeology make it clear that the city of Jericho was 3000 years old when Joshua crossed the Jordan. The modern scholars generally agree that this historical event belongs to the thirteenth century B.C. They have not as yet reached any agreement in explaining the collapse of Jericho's walls.

Scandal, to come to our third point, is often the result which follows the scholars' conclusions. To the question "What is the book of Job?" the scholar answers that it is a doctrinal and poetic dialogue. The questioner, unaccustomed to such answers and unprepared for them, may be shocked. Should the scholar be questioned about the Sermon on the Mount, he will probably answer that the evangelist has gathered together into a unified and orderly discourse a collection of teachings which were actually delivered at various times and in different places. This answer might

7

also be the occasion of scandal to those who errone-
ously feel that the Gospel writers are being accused of
writing fiction.

The question of scandal demands serious considera-
tion. For, if the public is shocked at the answers given
by scholars, and giving scandal is sinful, then perhaps
no answers should be offered. This is actually the
opinion of some people, namely that the scholar should
avoid, as far as possible, the occasions of doubt and
questioning, and should answer questions by appealing
to the general teaching of the Church. But this solution
is hardly realistic. In the first place, the scholars themselves are responsible for the present curiosity regarding
the Bible. They cannot simply withdraw now without
at least attempting to give the proper answers. Secondly,
if the scholars run away from the problems, the public
will only seek answers in another and perhaps more
dangerous direction.

I think the most sensible course is to try to devise
answers that will avoid surprise. More fundamentally
still, I think we must examine the causes of this kind
of scandal, and try to remove or counteract them. If
the answers to biblical problems cause any surprise, it
is because the public has not been prepared for them.
We must examine both the causes of, and the solutions
to, this lack of adequate preparation.

Sometimes the unnecessarily blunt formulation of
the answer is the reason for scandal. This can easily be

remedied by a liberal dose of charity and tact. More often, however, the public's wrong attitude, though inculpable, is the basis of the scandal. If such is the case, then the attitude must be corrected if scandal is to be avoided. This seems to involve a general orientation rather than a doubt about any particular problem. In these pages, therefore, I do not plan to solve any specific biblical questions (those concerning Adam's rib, the apple, the serpent, and so forth), but rather to outline a general attitude. The solution to concrete problems is an endless process; for every time we turn a page of the Bible, a new difficulty confronts us.

### THE MENTAL ATTITUDE

Once there was a man who suffered from a curious mental illness. He thought he heard within his head a little bird singing at the most inconvenient times: when he was trying to sleep, when he wanted to read, or when he tuned in on his favorite broadcast. He consulted many specialists, all of whom put him off with kind words or words perhaps not so kind. One day, however, he finally came to the right doctor. "Come to my office next Thursday morning," he was told. "I shall perform a simple little operation and remove the bird without pain." And so it happened. When the patient recovered from the light anesthetic, the doctor showed him a little bird beating its wings against the white sheet of his hospital bed. The man went home happy and satisfied, promising to return each week to report on the results of the operation. The following week he returned quite happy—"Marvelous, doctor! No more trouble at all!" Two weeks passed, and his joy and peace of mind continued. He could listen to Tschaikovsky without being disturbed, or hear Beethoven's *Pastoral Symphony* with no birds other than those the composer had put into the score. It was the same the third week. But on the twenty-fifth day he returned in great anguish. "But what could have happened?" asked the doctor. "You saw that I got the bird out." "Yes, doctor," the man replied, "but you left the nest inside."

Now in using this story as an analogy I do not insinuate that those with the problems we are speaking of are mentally ill; for just the opposite is true. Nevertheless there is a nest that shelters their difficulties and permits scandals to grow, and it is this I would try to remove. Once we have dealt with this attitude of mind, the state of shock will disappear. Then we can answer specific doubts without fear of the consequences, and we can even find it profitable to arouse further doubts. We shall thus have cancelled out the third part of our schema ("the public is scandalized") without changing the second part ("the scholar gives answers").

The resolution of the reader's difficulties, therefore, will be the first objective of the following pages. I will not answer any concrete problems, but will only attempt to form a correct attitude. Other authors, in books already published or yet to appear, can consider the specific problems. But I believe that the reader should begin with the proper orientation and thus prepare himself to read intelligently what is being written on this subject.

Is the situation we have been describing something new, or has it always existed? Has the problem arisen only with the biblical movement or the postwar period? And if it is something new, how did it come about? In this connection I am reminded of the passage in the *Spiritual Exercises* where St. Ignatius recommends to his priests that they avoid discussing the problem of predestination with "simple people," since they will only take scandal if offered a problem for which there is no solution: "Ordinarily we should not say a great deal about predestination, but if sometimes we do have occasion to refer to it, we should do so in such a way that the simple people will not fall into error, as sometimes happens" ("Rules for thinking with the Church," 15).

I am referring here only to the field of biblical studies and I do not of course consider the modern public to be made up of "simple people," that is, without much religious education. But even within the restricted field of biblical interpretation, can we say that the situation described is entirely new? To answer this question I will discuss three high points in biblical research, skipping over the intermediate stages. Since these high points are crucial, they can serve as signs of the total process and the general development which underlies them.

## THE FIRST STAGE:
### REFORMATION AND COUNTER REFORMATION

The first of these high points is the Reformation and Counter Reformation. This intellectual and polemical movement had a very great influence on biblical studies. The new movement failed, however, to attain new principles and methods of analysis, though Scholasticism had done this a few centuries before through the systematic application of dialectics. But they were able to make a spectacular advance with the aid of traditional methods.

### Protestant Reform

The Reformation was by no means a purely intellectual movement, nor did its interest in the Bible and its treatment of Scripture stem from a merely scientific zeal for study. Quite the contrary, the Protestant approach to and use of the Bible was avowedly controversial. Luther made a skillful translation of the Bible into German, but his treatment of Scripture was far less critical than that of St. Thomas Aquinas centuries before. Father Alberto Vaccari has compared the scriptural approaches of Luther and St. Thomas in a two-part article which appeared in *Civiltà cattolica*.[2] He cites several examples:

> Psalms 2 and 8, according to the Doctor of Wittenberg, are obvious prophecies of the passion and kingship of Christ. The Angelic Doctor, in explaining Psalm 2, applies the historical explanation to David and the mystical explanation to Christ. . . . St. Thomas explains Psalm 8 ("O Lord, our Lord, how glorious is your name over all the earth") as referring to the grandeur and goodness of God shining forth in every creature. Only at the end of his exposition, and then briefly and in a kind of appendix, does he point out how it can be applied to Christ: "These things can also be applied to the gifts of grace and thus all the mysteries of Christ are accounted among them."[3] This is said of a psalm which is cited three times in the New Testament as a witness to Christ! Here certainly St. Thomas is modern and Luther medieval. . . .
>
> Another example from the book of Isaiah. . . . In the beginning of Chapter 8, the prophet dramatically places before our eyes the conception and birth of a son whose prophetic name is Maher-shalal-hash-baz ("Speeding is the spoil, hastening the prey"). From this name he derives the prophecy that Judah's enemies, Damascus and Samaria, will soon be destroyed. This picture is comparable, point for point, with the

prophecy of Emmanuel, the son of a maiden, which is found in the preceding chapter and which is cited in the Gospel as an evident prophecy of the coming Christ. That is the principal, if not the sole reason, why the prophecy in the eighth chapter has been considered, or is now considered, to be strictly messianic in the literal sense. But St. Thomas explains it in a different way: "The Jews explain this literally as referring to the son of Isaiah."[4] He thus accepts as his own the Jewish interpretation of the passage. He does not pass over the difficulties in this interpretation, especially with regard to the striking parallel with Chapter 7. Here is his answer to the difficulty: "This explanation does not carry as much weight as the one above in Chapter 7 regarding the other sign (Emmanuel), for it is more forced and has no backing from the Scripture."[5] After answering the remaining difficulties, he continues confidently in his historical and literal interpretation, though he allows a typological interpretation: "It is not inappropriate, granting the literal sense of the passage, that the boy himself [the son of Isaiah] is a figure of Christ."[6]

Luther's commentary on this passage is much briefer and less clear. Over the name of the child he adds the marginal note: "Christ most worthily bears this title because of His death, whereby He robbed Hell." Then he adds later: "This is how the son of Isaiah derives his name."[7]

The Protestants affirmed one authority in order to deny another; for they set the authority of the Bible over against that of the Church. Thus the Bible, which inevitably became the sole basis of their faith, was converted into a polemical weapon.

In using this weapon, the tendency of early Protestantism was to regard everything in the Sacred Scriptures as inspired, right down to the last syllable, letter, and punctuation mark. The human author was looked upon as a merely passive instrument moved by the Holy Spirit. According to this way of thinking, it was irreligious to admit the existence of grammatical and linguistic mistakes in the sacred books. A person need not know Greek very well to realize how groundless this idea is, nor must he be an expert in Hebrew to reach the conclusion that the Bible has suffered with time, and that the language has been subject to the ordinary changes of linguistic development. In spite of this, the formula of faith accepted by the Protestants in Switzerland in 1676 (*Formula consensus Helvetica*) adopted a theory of inspiration consistent with this primitive Protestant tendency.[8]

Such an attitude was evidently prompted by respect for the Bible, even though the respect was exaggerated. It was also inspired by resistance to the Church. The Bible became a weapon for use in destroying the Church, or at least in defending theories and practices opposed to those of traditional Christianity.

Polemics may have the good effect of promoting the study of problems, but it often ends up by prejudicing and obscuring the solutions. By stirring up controversy, the Protestants actually promoted the study of Sacred Scripture on a grand scale. But their discoveries were often colored by their anti-Catholic bias and were predetermined by the confessions of faith which had been officially adopted as ultimate norms of interpretation. The practical result of their rejection of Church authority was the substitution of many new authorities. In its first century, Protestant exegesis could not boast of many outstanding biblical scholars. Luther, for example, leaned too heavily on typology, whereas Calvin was too literal in his interpretation. The rabbinical studies of Johannes Buxtorf are more valuable, as are the critical works of Hugo Grotius and the commentaries of Drusius (Jan van den Driessche).

## Catholic Reaction

The Catholic Church reacted vigorously to the Protestant Reformation with the great creative movement known as the Counter Reformation, a movement which dominated the entire sixteenth century. First and foremost the Church insisted emphatically on its own authority, which Protestantism had denied. It also maintained the authority of Scripture, but insisted that it should be interpreted according to tradition, and that the authorized interpreter of Scripture was the Catholic Church. The Church considers its authority to interpret Scripture an inalienable right, but this does not mean that Roman tribunals proceeded to multiply authoritative and definitive interpretations. Rather, the right of definitive interpretation is reserved for special cases. In ordinary cases, the Church allows full freedom to her scholars.

Since the Church was aware of the textual problems and the dangers of the times, she restricted the use and the reading of the Bible for the ordinary Catholic public. At the same time, the Church encouraged study and research among scholars. As a result ordinary Catholics were much less familiar with the Bible after the decrees of the Council of Trent than they had been before the Protestant Reformation.

In the article already mentioned, Father Vaccari cites a case which must have been typical in earlier times, namely a Spanish soldier who served as a prison guard in pre-Reformation Italy, and spent his spare time on duty reading the Bible. Further, the lists of medieval editions and translations of the Bible are very lengthy. In fact, all of medieval culture, its religion, art and literature, was permeated with Sacred Scripture. Nowadays no informed or sincere Protestant would attempt to revive the old calumny that the Church of the Middle Ages had kept the Bible from the people or had prevented translations into the vernacular languages.[9]

Although private Bible reading declined as a result of the Counter Reformation, the study of the Bible by Catholic scholars increased immeasurably. The Council of Trent ordered cathedral schools and colleges to set up chairs of biblical exegesis (*lectorales*) and to conduct courses in Sacred Scripture. Though the teachers used principles and study methods which differed little from those of past centuries, they did make some notable advances along the lines traced out by the great scholastic theologians. In the writer's own Spain, for example, we can cite the famous names of Arias Montano, distinguished for his wide factual knowledge of the Old Testament, Fray Luis de León, whose commentary on the *Song of Songs* is surprisingly modern, Maldonatus, the great commentator on the Gospels, Pineda, Mariana, Gaspar Sánchez, Alcázar and others. Hugo Hürter, in his *Nomenclator literarius*, cites more than four hundred Catholic interpreters of the Bible between 1564 and 1663.

With the advance of the seventeenth century, one notices a gradual decline which penetrates almost every field of human culture. The reasons for this would be difficult to define. The fact that the decline was general seems to indicate that no single cause was responsible. In the biblical field the tendency was to repeat the tried and safe positions without any effort of the creative imagination. Perhaps this was partially due to the prevalence of a narrow and rigid concept of orthodoxy. When such an attitude becomes dominant, the intellectual level inevitably sinks or is at least stifled in its development. In Spain the normal situation, namely the co-existence of a strict conservatism along with a more liberal viewpoint, can be seen in the case of the two great "Lions" of the sixteenth century, Fray Luis de León and León de Castro. But an increasing anti-Jewish influence encouraged by exaggerated orthodoxy brought about the decay of Hebraic studies which had previously flourished in Spain. With this decay biblical studies declined. There were of course other causes of decline, but this one was important and symptomatic.

Other movements, about which we shall speak later, made their appearance in the seventeenth century, but did not become influential at this time. Further, the eighteenth century witnessed the beginnings of the great spiritual upheavals which culminated in the magnificent scientific developments of the last century. This development we will now see in the study of the second of our historical crises.

### THE SECOND STAGE: RATIONALISM

*Protestant Reform*

History has given the name "the Enlightenment" to the movement which attempted the reappraisal of all truth in the light of critical objectivity. In the religious sphere Deism appeared, a naturalistic movement which would prune away men's fruitful supernatural branches. Then came Romanticism, which injected a vitality born of the tempestuous violence which the Germans called *Sturm und Drang*, "storm and stress." Compounded by new thinkers (Hamann, who lit the spark, Herder, the innovator of great genius, and the two Humboldt brothers, one of whom studied the natural sciences, *Naturwissenschaften*, while the other studied the sciences of the mind, *Geisteswissenschaften*), the product of these forces was the nineteenth century, especially as it developed in Germany. We are the heirs and descendents of that century's creative efforts.

In the biblical field Rationalism was intimately connected with these movements. From Romanticism it drew its insatiable curiosity and creative force, while from "enlightened" Positivism, it derived its methods of precise critical research. Great men and great works characterize the German Protestantism of the past century: Johann Gottfried Eichhorn, Wilhelm M. L. de Wette, Heinrich G. A. Ewald, Heinrich F. W. Gesenius, Julius Wellhausen and others, to mention only those prominent in the biblical field. As we enter into the twentieth century, we find still others, such as Hermann Gunkel and Hugo Gressmann.

These were men passionately dedicated to positive biblical research, men who possessed a wide range of knowledge and employed rigorous methodology. But as heirs of Deism, they were handicapped by a congenital defect: their rejection of the supernatural. Like a race of men whose ancestors had lost the ability to see color or hear music and had given birth to defective children, the Rationalist movement began by destroying its capacity to know or recognize the supernatural, and transmitted this defect to its descendents. No doubt they developed certain compensating virtues and their partial deafness and blindness were sometimes helpful in the critical examination of certain problems, but the defects were still fatal. And while it is true that their war on the supernatural resulted in the rejection of many unfounded pious beliefs, it also undermined what was most vital and essential to the Bible.

This point is brought out by Hermann Gunkel in his article, "Aims and Methods in the Interpretation of the Old Testament":

> If we lack the most important element of all in our criticism, we are only sounding brass and a tinkling cymbal; our power of observation is paralyzed and our love is frozen. What would we say of a man who has no appreciation for the beauty of music and yet undertakes to write on the history of music? Yet this is the exact situation when an irreligious man attempts to write on the history of religion or to interpret a religious book. The history of religion seems to be the only field where such a pretension is not openly scorned. We are forced by the facts themselves to assert that avowedly irreligious men, men who look upon religion as mere priestly humbug, . . . are often the ones who write with the greatest conviction on the history of religion. Obviously, if one begins with this outlook, only the strangest conclusions will be drawn.

We can only respond to such a man by saying that he is incapable of understanding the history of religion if he believes that its source is merely an interesting pathological phenomenon. Hence we insist that anyone who undertakes to interpret the Bible must be capable of grasping its religious content. He will be unable to do this unless he possesses within himself some element of the religious spirit he is studying.[10]

Unfortunately much of this paragraph could be quoted against Gunkel himself as well as against the whole Rationalist school. Their systematic denial of the supernatural (miracles, revelation, inspiration, special providence, sin, grace, redemption, prophecy) created a void which they tried to fill with explanations which in turn proved unsatisfactory. They caricatured the sublime teaching on the nature of grace and sin as portrayed in the Genesis account of the fall of man as the tale of a childish prank, *eines törichten Kinderstreiches*. Further, they explained the mystical experiences of the prophets as unusual but merely natural experiences which were to be understood in the light of pathological, or at least abnormal, psychology.

This rationalistic version of Protestantism was altogether different from that of the early Reformation. For the Reformers, the Bible had been a court of appeal to condemn the Catholic Church whenever it contradicted Protestant belief. But Rationalism moved in another direction, for Scripture was no longer regarded as having any divine authority, since its inspiration was one of the supernatural elements denied by the rationalists ("the beautiful myth of inspiration has been destroyed," said Gunkel). No longer could Scripture be a weapon against the Catholic Church, for it was simply a religious and literary document of unique significance, but entirely human in origin. As a matter of fact, Gunkel himself was responsible for bringing out with great skill the human values of biblical literature,

It might be thought that this new outlook on the Bible presented no serious danger for Catholics, since the Protestants no longer used the Bible as a polemical weapon, but rather, if anything, ignored the Catholics. Rationalism was, however, a serious threat to the Church on many counts.

In the first place the Church belongs entirely to a supernatural order—in its end and means, its foundation, destiny, doctrine, and sacraments. To deny this order is to deny the very possibility of salvation. Such a denial, therefore, has deadly consequences for all the institutions and members of the Church.

In addition, rationalistic biblical criticism could claim within its ranks an impressive array of learned and creative scholars. Their theories tended to receive the unqualified assent normally reserved to fully-proven conclusions. Their methodology and the fruits of their research, despite the fundamental errors of their system, continued to acquire an ever-wider influence. Against such a force, Catholic biblical scholarship was able to do very little. Rudolf Cornely and Joseph Knabenbauer took their stand firmly on tradition, Franz von Hummelauer and M.-J. Lagrange set out to explore new ideas with all the attendant risks. Little else was done. Rationalism had emerged like an immense mountain which overshadowed everything.

## The Apologetic Reaction

The reaction of Catholics was a typical one that occurs in times of grave danger: the Rationalist movement provoked apologetics. In the biblical field, as we can now survey it from a peaceful distance, this reaction impresses us mainly with its atmosphere of complete bewilderment. The apologetic attitude encouraged an extreme conservatism, sometimes to the disparagement of scientific accuracy. In their attack on Rationalism, men were blinded to the valid scientific conclusions which had been reached by Protestants. This attitude drew suspicion down on serious Catholic authors. At times they were denounced and attacked when they were only trying to understand and evaluate the valid conclusions. Thus a kind of civil war broke out among Catholics, driving the two sides even further apart, some going to extremes in their efforts to adopt the results of rationalist criticism, while others were just as extreme in their entire rejection of criticism. This controversy, which raged through the nineteenth and early twentieth centuries, wasted an enormous amount of energy when Catholics should have been united in a common cause.

Father Juan Prado, C.SS.R., has described for us some of the more significant aspects of this controversy.[11]

> The battle was not raging between Catholics and their adversaries. Rather, in Fr. Fonck's words, it was an internal war, a civil war.[12] This author did not look upon Catholic scholars as men who were all defending the same truth, each one according to his own talents and insights. Instead he saw them as members of two opposed camps, one of which was attacking and the other defending the truth of the Scripture . . . The core of the problem cannot be seen, he feels, until one mentions the work of Fathers Lagrange and von Hummelauer.[13]

Fr. Lagrange was at that time the most capable and best qualified of all the Catholic exegetes. When we look back on his life's work a half century later, we readily pass over his few mistakes in view of his many positive contributions. Some of his conclusions, premature for his time, are now fully accepted by Catholic exegetes, who are at present even more radical than Fr. Lagrange dared to be. His influence is still very much alive today.[14]

In Spain, Fr. Lino Murillo was a good example of the champions of extreme conservatism. His method seems to have been to interpret the words of Scripture in the most rigid way possible, with the result that he sometimes even deformed them. He seemed to be unaware of the principle stated by Pope Leo XIII in his encyclical, *Providentissimus Deus*, "that the biblical writers did not use scientific language, but spoke in figurative or popular speech, or according to appearances." He likewise ignored St. Augustine's principle, quoted by Pope Leo in the same encyclical, "that the sacred writers and the Holy Spirit did not intend to teach men in the Bible the essential nature of the visible universe, which was in no way relevant to salvation." For, according to Fr. Murillo, the Bible conveys to us "truths dealing with the same subject matter as the natural sciences, to the end that we should be instructed in them in the dogmatic as well as the scientific order, the exclusive basis of our assent being the divine authority and affirmation." He amplified this idea with some concrete instances:

> The origin of the human organism and of the animals and plants, the unicity or plurality of the first beginnings of human life, and so forth, are in these days objects of earnest study on the part of the natural sciences. But it is incontestable that the Scripture contains concrete instructions concerning every one of these matters, to the end that the faithful should know about them. Now if such truths were proposed in the Bible only in the guise of simple appearances and not in keeping with reality, such sections of the biblical text would be in part deceitful, in part entirely useless. These truths would in such a case be subject ex-

clusively to the judgment of science, which is unknown by the vast majority of mankind and which is constantly being changed by those who do know it.

For the polemic animus of Fr. Murillo, the name von Hummelauer was interchangeable with Modernism.[15]

I have heard those who knew him tell of Fr. Murillo that it was his habit to alternate the reading of Protestant and Catholic biblical works; for he recognized the persuasive force of the Protestant works. As a matter of fact, Protestant authors of the time were guilty of more serious errors than were the Catholics, but their scientific method was superior.

As for the civil war among Catholics, Fr. Lagrange was not incorrect when he retorted to Fr. Fonck's depreciation of the Catholic authors of the "progressive bloc": "It will have to be conceded that virtually all who have written biblical works esteemed by the public would prefer to be numbered among the progressives than among their opponents."

The reaction just described was far different from that evoked by early Protestantism. At the time of the Reformation, there existed a threat complicated by a spreading revolt, but the Catholic intellectual reaction was fruitful as well as vigorous. Catholic biblical writers were capable and respected. When the initial vigor of their reaction subsided, there emerged an attitude which was conservative but positive.

At the end of the last century, however, the Catholic

reaction was defensive. The dissensions among Catholic scholars were much more than mere academic debates. In the sixteenth century, it was taken for granted that a Catholic author would fall into occasional errors in the attempt to find answers to new problems. All that was demanded of them was to retract their mistakes and then go on with their work. This very thing happened twice to Suárez with reference to his teaching on auricular confession. After the pope had condemned his teaching, the Spanish theologian offered an interpretation of the papal decree and then submitted to this view of it. Once again the Pope intervened, declaring that Suárez had misinterpreted his words. The Spanish theologian submitted again. But none of this byplay interfered with his normal activity of study, teaching, and writing. It was taken for granted that positive action was more important than the danger of occasional error, and obedience was not regarded as a merely passive virtue. As a result, Catholic intellectual activity went on unimpaired.

But biblical studies at the end of the last century were overshadowed by fear: fear of possible errors among Catholics, fear of the contagion of Rationalism and Modernism, fear of compromising the integrity of revelation and the value of the sacred books. The fear was well grounded, no doubt, for there was a real and present danger. But it also arose from the technical and scholarly inadequacies of Catholic scholars taken as a whole, at least in comparison with the Protestants. Nobody admitted this fact publicly, but it was certainly felt, at least subconsciously.

## Restrictive Measures

The reaction of the Church to this situation took two forms, one of them the exercise of a restrictive discipline, the other the encouragement of serious study and training.

To the first category belong the decrees of the Biblical Commission, which imposed a firm control over all opinions to be defended or published, but insisted that this study be accompanied by a complete submission to the authority of the Church. Since the application of these disciplinary norms was strict, some now maintain that they were too rigid, so that the freedom necessary for the critical study of Scripture was seriously hampered. Regarding this opinion, I would like to cite two rather interesting comments.

The first comment is by a Protestant recognized as an eminent authority for his many scholarly contributions in the fields of archaeology, history, and biblical philology. I refer to Professor William F. Albright, who used these words in presenting the work of a Catholic author to the Protestant public:

> The Responsa of the Pontifical Biblical Commission with regard to the limits of critical enquiry in the Old Testament field were issued between 1905 and 1910,

after prolonged study on the part of an eminent committee, weighted rather heavily, as might be expected in such a serious ecclesiastical matter, on the conservative side. As is well known, some of the so-called Modernists, such as Loisy, had moved so far to the left in their criticism that more orthodox Catholics were scandalized and a strong reaction set in. The reviewer, as a convinced Protestant, believes that the reaction went too far and that the Responsa were too narrow in their decisions. However, they put a check to the excesses in literary and historical criticism which were rapidly spreading from Protestant to Catholic circles. As a result Catholic O.T. scholarship has been pretty free from the unparalleled effusion of futility which has been characteristic of Protestant scholarship in this field during the past half century. Nor does the reviewer wish to deny either the positive or the negative value of a considerable fraction of O.T. research in non-Catholic circles!

Albright wrote these words in 1947, when reviewing a book by Msgr. Steinmüller.[16]

The second comment I wish to cite was written in 1955 on the occasion of the publication of the second official edition of the *Enchiridion biblicum*. Athanasius Miller, O.S.B., then secretary of the Biblical Commission, wrote the following words which may be regarded as semiofficial:

It is hard for us now to imagine the situation in which Catholic professors found themselves at the turn of the century or the dangers in which the Catholic doctrine of the inspiration of Scripture was involved when the current of liberal and rationalistic criticism threatened to sweep away all the safeguards of tradition then held in reverential awe. Now that the turmoil has died down substantially, and many of the old controversies have been quietly abandoned, while other problems now present themselves in an entirely different light, it may be easy to smile at the "narrowness" and "restrictions" which prevailed at that time.[17]

Both the Protestant and the Catholic professor agree, therefore, that this situation must be viewed in its proper historical perspective. They also agree that it is a situation which belongs to the past, not to the present.

## Constructive Measures

Naturally, Church authority was not content with merely laying down restrictions. It also took positive steps to encourage Bible study and the training of various kinds of specialists. In 1886 M.-J. Lagrange, O.P., had founded the École biblique de Jérusalem. It was officially opened for studies in 1890. Two years later it began to publish the *Revue biblique,* and its highly respected series of *Études bibliques* was started in 1900. In a letter of September 17, 1892, Pope Leo XIII gave his approval to Fr. Lagrange's work:

> If your plans and their realization have earned the justifiable praise of all those who have a scholarly interest in these studies, then surely you should not fail to receive praise from Us, Who consider these studies to be of the utmost importance, to be furthered

and encouraged on every occasion. Take courage, beloved son, in this noble and useful enterprise, difficult though it may be, and may all those who have joined you under our authority and with our approval take courage.[18]

The following year, 1893, this same pope published his great encyclical *Providentissimus Deus* for the encouragement and direction of biblical studies. In 1909 St. Pius X founded the Pontifical Biblical Institute for scriptural research and for the training of future professors of Scripture. In the document erecting the Institute the pope insisted on the role of technical training in biblical study: ". . . practical training in every aspect of biblical erudition . . . let them be aided by all the means which they feel studies and labors of this type require . . . biblical learning and all the studies related to it . . . lectures and exercises on particular problems relating to interpretation, introduction, archaeology, history, geography, philology, and other disciplines relevant to the sacred books."[19]

Before passing to the third stage of our treatment, I should pause to bring out an important point. The attitude of many present-day Catholics, and this includes many priests still in the active ministry, was formed during the period of Rationalism and the apologetics that opposed it. The professors of that day transmitted their attitude to their students, and the priests who were educated at that time popularized the same attitude in their sermons and instructions. Books which are still on our bookshelves and are still read today were written in the same spirit. As is normal in the process of cultural development, the attitude began at the top and gradually descended to and penetrated the popular level. Many present-day Catholics, therefore, due to their training, their teachers, and their reading, still maintain the attitude which was a reaction against the Rationalist attack.

This way of thinking has perhaps not lasted so long in Germany because the people maintained closer contact with the Bible.[20] It certainly has not persisted in France, where it has been all but abandoned. But one encounters it frequently in Spain, Italy, England, Ireland, and the United States, where the new attitudes demanded by the changing times have not yet been widely popularized.

## THE THIRD STAGE: THE PRESENT

We now come to the third stage, in which we are living today. The "magna charta" of this age is the encyclical of Pius XII, *Divino afflante Spiritu*. The scripture scholar realizes the full value of this pontifical directive, the effects of which have only reached the Catholic public in part and in an indirect way. Professor Albright himself, in the review from which I quoted above, has this to say about the encyclical:

As is gradually becoming known in non-Catholic circles, there is in progress a tremendous movement for the vulgarization of the Bible, that is, for the translation of the Bible into the vernaculars and the widest possible diffusion of Scripture among the Catholic masses. The best official directives for the biblical movement will be found in the papal encyclical, *Divino Afflante Spiritu,* issued in 1943. In this historic document equal attention is devoted to the encouragement of biblical scholarship, including intensive philological and archaeological research in ancillary fields, and to the promotion of the use of the Bible for devotional and liturgical purposes.[21]

This encyclical, which was published in September of 1943, was the fulfillment of a long process and many years of study. The constructive measures taken at the beginning of the century now bore fruit and one of the results was the possibility of loosening restrictive measures which had been imposed. It is in this new atmosphere that most of those now active in the biblical field were trained, and in this new atmosphere the biblical movement of today has grown up and expanded. I shall now attempt to describe some of the more important aspects of this new situation.

## The Conquest of Rationalism

In the first place a profound change has occurred within Protestantism: Rationalism as a movement has been conquered. This does not mean that the movement is dead, but only that it has been controlled and as-similated. Thanks in large measure to the monumental work of the Protestant theologian, Karl Barth, Rationalism as a determining force in religion is largely a thing of the past. There are still many Rationalists and they still use Rationalist principles in their biblical research, but the solid Rationalist front has been broken. Though they disagree in their explanations of them, or avoid explanations entirely, many Protestant scholars nowadays accept the inspiration of Scripture, the reality of miracles, and so forth.

One of the leading scripture scholars of England, H. H. Rowley, wrote in this fashion a few years ago:

> ... it is sometimes alleged that critical scholarship is based on the denial of the possibility of miracle (Cf. *The New Bible Handbook*, ed. by G. T. Manley, 2nd ed., 1949, pp. 40ff., where it is argued that modern critical scholarship is based on, and permeated by, unbelief in the possibility of miracle). Let me say with clarity and candour that I am a critical scholar and that I neither begin nor end with any such denial. If miracle be defined as divine activity within the world, a belief in its possibility would seem to be fundamental to a belief in God. He cannot be excluded from the world he has made, or reduced to the position of a spectator of the interplay of forces which he had once set in motion. In the faith of Israel he was too real and personal to be reduced to impotence in his own world, or regarded as one who idly watched while men worked out their own destiny, and this faith is integral to any

worth-while faith in God. Many of the miracles recorded in the Old Testament are examples of divine activity through natural events, such as the deliverance from Egypt through wind and wave, from Sisera through storm, or from Sennacherib through plague. Others are examples of divine activity through events which were contrary to the order of Nature, such as the passage through walls of water at the Red Sea, the standing still of the sun in the time of Joshua, the recovery of an axe-head by Elisha by the device of throwing wood into the water, or the delivery of the three youths from Nebuchadnezzar's fire. In some cases these stories are dramatic representations of simpler facts, as may be seen by a study of the context in which they are set; or wonder tales that grew round the name of a hero; or parabolic stories that were made the vehicle of a message. The miracle stories can neither be uncritically accepted as historical, nor uncritically rejected as fancy. Each example must be examined for itself, in the light of the character of the narrative in which it stands and the purpose for which it appears to have been written. But that there is a truly miraculous element in the story I am fully persuaded. We have not merely the working out of human impulses and the chance interplay of natural forces. We have the activity of God in inspiration and revelation, and the evidence of his presence in Nature and history.[22]

This conquest of Rationalism in the biblical field is only part of a much broader movement in all of Western culture, which is not only receptive to, but even eager for the marvelous, the mysterious, the preternatural, the subconscious, and so forth. Such a movement will inevitably involve some exaggerations and corruptions, but I am only concerned here with the positive contribution it can make to our culture. Twentieth century man has recovered the use of faculties which were sacrificed to reason in the nineteenth century and many Protestant scripture scholars now seem to have rediscovered what is most profound about the Bible, and what Catholics have always clung to with such tenacity.

## Critical Moderation

Besides the radical correction we have just seen, the conquest of Rationalism, we must also note the wholehearted change of attitude among Protestant critics regarding the historical and scientific values of the books of the Old Testament. Textual criticism has lost some of its brashness and literary criticism is more cautious and humble. How different is the attitude of a present-day commentator on Isaiah from the coldly surgical criticism employed by Duhm a half century ago! In 1901 Bernhard Duhm stated with absolute confidence that Jeremiah had written nothing in prose. On this criterion he decided which were the authentic utterances of the prophet. W. Rudolph, in 1947, rejected Duhm's criterion but accepted his conclusions. A. Weiser, in 1955, maintained that the disputed passages are authentic, and O. Eissfeldt, in 1956, went along with this theory. In 1924 G. Hölscher denied to Ezekiel more than half of the book attributed to him. C. C. Torrey, in 1930, took away the entire book, calmly moving its date up to the third century B.C., whereas Ezekiel lived during the seventh and sixth centuries B.C. In 1936 however, A. Bertholet had already begun restoring the book to Ezekiel, and this interpretation prevails today, setting aside, of course, those elements commonly admitted to be retouches, additions, and elaborations.

As early as 1930 a new trend could be seen in historical criticism. It consisted of a genuine "reconquest" of the historicity of the Bible following the lines laid down by Albrecht Alt and his school. While reviewing an important work of this period, H. W. Hertzberg wrote:

> The scientific study of the Old Testament is now engaged in reconquering areas that had been wholly or practically abandoned. Many things which were previously considered to be additions in a prophetic text, for example, are now considered to be authentic (cf. the new commentary by Procksch on Isaiah or Cramer's on Amos). On the problem of the Servant of Yahweh, the messianic interpretation is now returning to the center of interest and merits serious attention (Rudolph, Vischer). The Patriarchs have recovered a recognizable historical character (Böhl), and their "religion" is not only admitted but even considered to be of great importance for the history of religions

(Alt). Moses has long since been recalled from the twilight of legend (Gressmann, Sellin). The Law and the Psalms are no longer regarded as products of a late period of decadence. In a word, tradition has regained its respectability. In this context belongs Noth's book (The System of the Twelve Tribes of Israel). The area which he has re-evaluated is that of the period of the Judges. . . . The key to his discoveries is to be found in what can be called his "traditio-historical method."[23]

Moreover, an ever-growing number of Protestant scholars is now prepared to admit the transcendent significance of the Old Testament. According to H. Gunkel at the beginning of this century, the Old Testament was only an important document in the study of religious history. It was important because the religion of Israel held a special significance among the ancient religions, and the documents of Israel's religion were the books of the Old Testament. Therefore the student of religious history must examine these books carefully, though he need not find in them any meaning for himself personally.

The modern Protestant scholar, on the other hand, when studying the theology of the Old Testament, insists not only on its concrete historical context but also on its enduring religious value. An entire series of commentaries now nearing completion is devoted specifically to the religious message of the sacred books of the Old Testament (I refer to *Das Alte Testament Deutsch*, published in Göttingen. Its counterpart for the New

*39*

Testament also exists, *Das Neue Testament Deutsch*).

In short, a Catholic today who makes use of the scriptural work of Protestants will be rewarded with a more profitable, positive, and respectful treatment than would have been the lot of his scholarly counterpart fifty years ago. Hence it is only natural that the Catholic specialist in Scripture has now adopted a new attitude toward the writings of Protestants. No longer does he maintain at the outset an attitude of suspicion, his mind closed on principle. He does not have the attitude of the customs inspector who expects to find poison, contraband, and subversive material on every page. Rather it is the attitude of a tester of merchandise whose primary interest is the quality of the article. This way of thinking is altogether more profitable for the cause of study and research.

## Attitudes toward Catholics

Protestant scripture scholars a half century ago made a point of overlooking the work of their Catholic colleagues. The rule was *catholica non leguntur*, "what is Catholic is not worth reading." If the rule had been simply an unconscious one, we could say that they were ignorant of Catholic biblical scholarship or were simply not interested in it. But the rule was a conscious one and must be interpreted as rather haughty contempt, hardly justified by the superiority the Protestants enjoyed in scientific achievement. "The Roman

Catholic Church has done its utmost to cut the nerve of historical exegesis," wrote Thomas K. Cheyne in 1886, who summed up his attitude to Catholic exegetes in the words of Dante: "Let us not speak of them, but look, and pass on." Catholics, as we have seen, were much more liberal on the other side, even including Father Murillo, who would include an occasional Catholic among the Protestant authors he condemned. The situation has now changed radically.

The change in attitude was expressed externally and officially in 1935 (we have already seen how Hertzberg indicated the change among Protestants in 1931). That year German scripture scholars were holding a congress. The director of the congress, J. Hempel, sent an invitation to the Pontifical Biblical Institute in Rome. The Rector of the Institute, Augustin Bea, S.J. (now Cardinal Bea, President of the Secretariat for Promoting Christian Unity for the Second Vatican Council), brought the matter before Pope Pius XI. The pope not only gave him permission to attend but urged other professors to attend and to take an active part in the meeting. As a result 35 Catholics attended the congress, together with some 70 Protestants. When one of the Protestant delegates had finished delivering a paper on the subject of inspiration, Fr. Bea rose to declare that the opinion expressed in the paper was in no way contrary to Catholic teaching on inspiration. He explained that since the same Holy Spirit inspired both the Old and New Testaments, they could not contradict but only complement one another. Otto Procksch was quite pleased at this and stated that up to that time he had not heard this Catholic belief explained.

In the last session of the congress, Fr. Bea, in virtue of his office as rector of the Institute, was invited to preside over the closing of the congress.

This meeting was undoubtedly of historic significance. Among the Catholics who took an active part in it, we read the names of A. Bea, F. Stummer, J. Fischer and H. Junker. Among those also present were A. Miller (the former secretary of the Biblical Commission), J. Hofbauer (now a professor at Innsbruck), J. B. Schildenberger (a professor in Beuron), G. Closen, S. Landersdorfer (now a bishop), A. Pohl (former dean of the Oriental Faculty of the Biblical Institute), E. F. Sutcliffe, J. Ziegler and others. In those days international congresses were not as common as they are today (at this meeting one of the papers was in French and several in English). The German scholars moreover were universally regarded with the deepest respect.

Almost twenty years later the British Society for Old Testament Study, composed mostly of Protestant denominations, decided to hold its annual meeting at the Pontifical Biblical Institute in Rome. That year the president was an English Catholic, Msgr. G. A. Barton. On the dais of the main auditorium of the Institute, Catholic, Protestant and Jewish speakers appeared in succession, united in their dedication to Sacred Scripture.

In 1934 Otto Eissfeldt first published his universally respected introduction to the Old Testament, in which the number of Catholic authors cited was rather small. But in 1956 the second edition came out with an index in which we find the names of many Catholic exegetes: R. Brown, E. Bruns, J. Fitzmyer, G. Glanzman, J. McKenzie, R. Murphy, P. Skehan and B. Vawter (among the Americans); still others, who were cited many times, such as J. Ziegler (17 times), J. van der Ploeg (15 times), H. Junker and E. Vogt (13 times), J. Coppens (11 times), A. Bea and F. M. Abel (10 times), R. de Vaux (12 times), and many others. At the International Congress of Orientalists held in Munich in 1957, Eissfeldt's seventieth birthday was honored in a special ceremony, which included greetings from the Catholic Biblical Association of America and the Dominican École biblique de Jérusalem. At the annual meeting of the Society of Biblical Literature and Exegesis in New York in December of 1958, this predominantly Protestant group voted to exchange delegates with the Catholic Biblical Association at its annual meeting.

Fifty years ago the Old Testament was a battleground in the war fought between Protestant Rationalists and Catholic apologists, or between conservative and liberal Catholics. Today the Old Testament is a field of labor on which sincere students can meet without acrimony to work in a common cause.

Today there can exist a periodical such as *Vetus Testamentum*, published in Holland, open in equal measure to the contributions of Catholics, Protestants, and Jews. There is no other requirement except that the contributions maintain high scholarly standards. Doctrinal differences, of course, are still recognized. Protestants, or at least the majority of them, have been converted to the genuine historical and religious meaning of the Old Testament, but they have not been converted to Catholicism. Catholics are now more open to new theories and methods but have not renounced their Catholicism or their spirit of obedience to the Church's directives and instructions. This spirit of obedience to the Church still radically differentiates the Catholic and Protestant approach to the Bible. Floyd V. Filson has expressed this difference quite well in a recent book: "Any Protestant who never tests or examines his own confession or that of his Church by the standard of Scripture, and who fails to keep clear that what he believes and what his Church confesses is secondary to Scripture, is a Roman Catholic at heart. He is ascribing controlling authority to his Church and its tradition."[24]

But this radical difference need not impede collaboration in all good will. The present atmosphere of cooperation is undoubtedly preferable from the point of view of productive scholarship. It would be unthinkable to return to the situation now past, when some scholars won their laurels as dauntless defenders of orthodoxy in brave intellectual contests, but their efforts failed to advance the knowledge of Scripture. Research is the task of quiet men and receives little help from those who fancy themselves heroic polemicists. Polemics did not pave the way to our present situation. Rather it was the obscure Catholic scholar who worked diligently in the spirit of humble obedience, sometimes little appreciated or understood, but patiently hopeful. We are the heirs of their labor through no efforts of our own. Those of us who began work in the field only a few years ago have been able to make use of a rich fund of Catholic scholarly productions and an atmosphere of peace in which work is possible. It would be foolish and vain if we were to take the merits of their labors upon ourselves, just as it would be rash and ungrateful to try turning back the clock to the point where they began.

We live in a new era which marks the terminal point of their efforts, an era which has been opened and approved in the encyclical of Pope Pius XII:

> It is right and pleasing to confess openly that it is not only by reason of these initiatives, precepts and exhortations of Our Predecessors that the knowledge and use of the Sacred Scriptures have made great progress

among Catholics; for this is also due to the works and labors of all those who diligently cooperated with them, both by meditating, investigating and writing, as well as by teaching and preaching and by translating and propagating the Sacred Books. . . .

From these, therefore, and from other initiatives which daily become more widespread and vigorous, as, for example, biblical societies, congresses, libraries, associations for meditation on the Gospels, We firmly hope that in the future reverence for, as well as the use and knowledge of, the Sacred Scriptures will everywhere more and more increase for the good of souls. . . .

There is no one who cannot easily perceive that the condition of biblical studies and their subsidiary sciences has greatly changed within the last fifty years. [Archaeology, inscriptions, codices, etc.] . . . All these advantages which, not without a special design of Divine Providence, our age has acquired, are, as it were, an invitation and inducement to interpreters of the Sacred Literature to make diligent use of this light, so abundantly given, to penetrate more deeply, explain more clearly and expound more lucidly the Divine Oracles. . . .

It is scarcely necessary to observe that this criticism [textual], which some fifty years ago not a few made use of quite arbitrarily and often in such a way that one would think they did so to introduce into the sacred text their own preconceived ideas, today has rules so firmly established and secure that it has become a most valuable aid. . . .

Moreover, we may rightly and deservedly hope that our times can also contribute something towards the deeper and more accurate interpretation of Sacred Scripture. For not a few things, especially in matters pertaining to history, were hardly at all or at least not fully explained by the commentators of past ages, since they lacked almost all the information which was needed for their clearer exposition. . . . Quite wrongly, therefore, do some maintain, incorrectly understanding the conditions of biblical study, that nothing remains to be added by the Catholic exegete of our time to what Christian antiquity has produced. On the contrary, these our times have brought to light so many things which call for a fresh investigation and a new examination, and which stimulate not a little the practical zeal of the present-day interpreter. . . .

As in our age new questions and new difficulties are multiplied, so, by God's favor, new means and aids to exegesis are also provided.[25]

The same pope who opened up the new age, Pius XII, could later look back with great satisfaction on the fifteen years of study that had gone by. Six weeks before he died, Pius wrote these words to the Catholic scripture scholars reunited at the great congress of Louvain:

To Our very dear Son, Cardinal Joseph-Ernest van Roey, Archbishop of Malines:

We are most willing to grant the wish which you expressed to Us in favor of the participants in the International Biblical Congress which will be held next month from August twenty-fifth to thirtieth at the "Civitas Dei" Pavilion of the Brussels World Exhibition, and through you, dearest Son, We address this personal Message to them.

Since the beginning of Our Pontificate, We have had close to Our heart the intention of fostering the growth of Scripture studies, and it is now almost fifteen years since We desired by Our Encyclical, *Divino afflante Spiritu*, "to incite ever more earnestly all those sons of the Church who devote themselves to these studies" and to encourage them "to continue with ever renewed vigor, with all zeal and care, the work so happily begun" (*Div. Aff. Spir.*, pp. 259, 282). Further, you are well aware that We have not ceased to pour out lavishly the marks of Our interest on the commentators and professors of Sacred Scripture.

Therefore We are happy to express our fatherly interest to the Catholic teachers who will soon be reunited at Brussels in order to pool together the riches of their knowledge and promote the progress of all the sciences necessary for a better understanding of the sacred text. Docile to the Church, the guardian and interpreter of Sacred Scripture, and encouraged by Our regard for their austere but extremely important task, may they continue their studies with confidence; for in this way "they will contribute most efficaciously to the salvation of souls, to the progress of the Catholic faith, to the honor and glory of God, and they will perform a work most closely connected with the apostolic office" (*Div. Aff. Spir.*, p. 281). As a pledge of the outpouring of divine grace on your labors, We wholeheartedly grant to them and also to you, dearest Son, the interpreter of their filial sentiments, Our very fatherly Apostolic Benediction.

*Vatican City, July 28, 1958*[26]

## The Training of Catholic Scholars

Catholic scholars have also experienced a change of attitude within the past fifty years, but not in the same way as the Protestants. The fundamental change, I believe, consists in the better scientific training they have been receiving. It would be unfair to ask whether there exists today a Catholic biblical scholar of the stature of Cornely or Lagrange. No one could answer such a question at this time. But there can be no doubt that Catholic professors and students of the Bible now receive a normal training far superior to that of fifty years ago. Progress here is sure and evident, a sequel to the positive measures adopted at the beginning of the century. What might have at first appeared to be a quantitative change (more specialists, more preparation), has actually resulted in a qualitative change, something characteristic of Catholic study today as a whole.

There are many obvious examples at hand to bring out this superior technical training. Ten years ago the best biblical atlas was *The Westminster Historical Atlas to the Bible*, the work of two Protestant scholars, F. V. Filson and G. E. Wright. Today two biblical atlases share the honor of being considered the best, each with its own particular features. Both are the work of Catholics, *Atlante storico della Bibbia* by D. Baldi and P. Lemaire, and *Atlas of the Bible* by L. H.

Grollenberg. The latter book was prepared with the collaboration of a Protestant scholar and was translated into English by two Protestants, J. M. H. Reid and H. H. Rowley.

Years ago the Society of Sciences of the University of Göttingen undertook the task of publishing a critical edition of the Greek translation of the Old Testament known as the Septuagint. It was to appear in a series of volumes. Since the twenties, the work was under the direction of the distinguished Protestant scholar, A. Rahlfs. After Rahlfs' death and the incidental interruption of the work for various reasons, it has now been entrusted to a Catholic professor, Fr. J. Ziegler. Thus a project begun by Protestants has with the passage of time come into the charge of a Catholic, simply because he was recognized as the highest authority on this subject.

*The* biblical discovery of this century was the set of documents found in caves near the Dead Sea. On the international team devoted to the reconstruction and publication of these manuscripts, Catholic scholars have played a principal role. Especially deserving of mention are Fathers Roland de Vaux, O.P., J. T. Milik, J. Starcky, and Msgr. P. W. Skehan.

I am not comparing the relative merits of present-day Catholic and Protestant exegetes. Rather I am comparing the Catholic scholars of today with their predecessors. There can be no doubt that today Catholic scholars as a body are superior to those of fifty years ago. Thus the desires and hopes of Leo XIII and St. Pius X have been realized:

> The progressive exploration of the antiquities of the East, the more accurate examination of the original text itself, the more extensive and exact knowledge of languages both biblical and Oriental, have, with the help of God, happily provided the solution of not a few of those questions which, in the time of Our Predecessor Leo XIII of immortal memory, were raised by critics outside or hostile to the Church against the authenticity, antiquity, integrity and historical value of the Sacred Books. For Catholic exegetes, by a right use of those same scientific arms, not infrequently misused by the adversaries, proposed interpretations which are in harmony with Catholic doctrine and the genuine current of tradition, while at the same time they are known to have proved equal to the difficulties, either those raised by new explorations and discoveries, or those bequeathed by antiquity for solution in our time.

> Thus it has come about that confidence in the authority and historical value of the Bible, though somewhat shaken in the minds of some by so many attacks, is completely restored today among Catholics; moreover, there are even some non-Catholic writers who by serious and calm inquiry have been led to abandon modern opinions and to return, at least in some points, to the more ancient ideas. This change is due in great part to the untiring labor by which Catholic commentators of the Sacred Letters, in no way deterred by difficulties and obstacles of all kinds, strove

with all their strength to make suitable use of what learned men of the present day, by their investigations in the fields of archaeology or history or philology, have made available for the solution of new questions.[27]

## Peace and Confidence

The improved technical preparation has brought with it confidence and serenity, the necessary climate for worthwhile study. This undisturbed calm is needed by the scholar if he is to be able to test new hypotheses, correct old theories, revise and reconstruct. Such a climate has been the normal experience of Catholic scholars in this third stage of our history.

As we have already seen, however, the attitude of a large part of the Catholic public was formed during the former apologetic age. The result has been a great division among Catholics. It is only natural that there should be a lag of some years between the research of scholars and the assimilation of this research by the public. But it is not normal and by no means desirable that the mentalities of the two should be so far apart. But they are indeed apart, and this is the source of many of our present-day difficulties.

The public demands information of the scholar according to *its* way of thinking, and the scholar answers according to *his* way of thinking. Failing to understand, the public is often shocked. The remedy for this is not that the scholar should adopt an attitude which was fortunately discarded years ago. Rather the solution is for the public to reform its attitude and to realize the actual facts of the present situation. These facts we shall see in the following pages.

# Chapter II.
# Biblical Criticism

Though most of the public is divided in its thinking between a naïve trust in the Bible and a "concordistic" attitude which would avoid all questioning of the Bible, both Protestant and Catholic biblical scholars have nevertheless developed a highly critical attitude. A half century ago many Catholic scholars described exegetes of the Protestant school as "critics," some adding the words "independent" or "radical." For some scholars this varied manner of expression pointed up their distrust in criticism, while for others it merely indicated a desire to limit the extension of the word "criticism." Nowadays, when little remains of the old polemical attitude, the majority of Catholic biblical scholars are trained in the theory and methods of criticism, and profess at the same time to be loyal to the Church and obedient to its teaching authority.

### ANTICRITICAL SCHOOLS

One might well ask at this point how anyone can subject the sacred books of the Bible to criticism, if it is one of the distinct privileges of the sacred to be untouchable. Consecrated hands may touch what is sacred, once they have undergone the proper rites of purification, but how can they subject it to criticism? The only fitting attitude when one is confronted by the sacred words of the Bible is that of the reverent hearer. To criticize such a book is to desecrate it, to strip it of its numinous quality. Surely this is sacrilegious.

The rabbinical school known as the "pilpulists" actually adopted such an exaggerated approach to biblical criticism.[1] They felt that *everything* in the Bible was sacred, including the shape and numerical values of the letters. They would draw hidden and strange interpretations, for example, by rearranging the letters of a word to correspond with the reversed letters of the alphabet (first and last, second and second-to-last, third and third-to-last, and so forth). The famous rabbi Aqiba-ben-Joseph was the foremost member of this school. The pilpulists' material symbolism and fantastic approach to the Bible would consign scriptural interpretation to the vagueness of mere cabalistic conjecture.

Some seventeenth-century Protestants with conservative leanings adopted a different approach, but made the Bible equally intangible. They held the theory that everything in the Bible, including commas and accents, is inspired in the sense that it is immediately dictated by God. According to this theory the human author could hardly be more than a mechanical secretary. The Imagist school led by Johann Koch (1603–

1669) employed this theory to discover symbols and tropes in every corner of the sacred text.[2] Further, since the Bible was the absolute norm of religious authority for Protestantism, they forbade any critical tampering with the sacred books.[3]

Catholic biblical scholars never endorsed such extreme theories as these. In contrast to the rabbinical school, the Fathers of the Church manifested a balanced and critical attitude toward the Bible. This can be seen in men of differing temperaments: St. Jerome, who was objective and scientific in his thinking, St. Augustine, who loved the mystical and sublime, Origen, noted for his allegorizing tendency, and St. Thomas, who strove for order and clarity. The best of the Catholic biblical commentators who wrote after the council of Trent also preserved an accurate and reasonable critical attitude toward the sacred text.

It is still true to say, however, that criticism, in the proper and technical sense of the word, is a movement which began in the second half of the seventeenth century. It was a movement of such novelty and importance that it actually failed against the traditionalist school which had so long held biblical interpretation in its grip.

One can best view this movement through some of its publications: the *Critici sacri* of 1660, which was a collection of Protestant and Catholic biblical commentaries, and the *Synopsis criticorum sacrorum*, a compendium of commentaries which appeared in 1669. It is interesting to note how the word "sacred" in the title of the last book cited can be applied to criticism. This implies the legitimacy of employing criticism in studying the sacred books, while they do not for that reason cease to be sacred or authoritative.

In the seventeenth century, however, criticism was hardly more than the name of a new movement. This movement only became powerful upon the publication in 1650 of *Critica sacra*, written by the Protestant biblical scholar, Louis Cappelli, and of a whole series of books by the Catholic priest, Richard Simon: *Histoire critique du texte, des versions, et des commentateurs du Vieux Testament* (1678, 1680, 1681), *Histoire critique du Nouveau Testament* (1689), *Histoire critique des versions du Nouveau Testament* (1690), *Histoire critique des principaux commentateurs du Nouveau Testament* (1693), *Nouvelles observations sur le texte et les versions du Nouveau Testament* (1695), and still other apologetic works which were published under a pen name.

## RICHARD SIMON

Though the scope of this book only allows for a brief outline of his career, this great genius really deserves a full biography.[4] His great interest in languages and independent study began during his undergraduate days in college. Latin was then taught as the basic language but Simon applied himself especially to Greek out of personal preference. While he was studying theology at the Sorbonne, he lost interest in the dry speculations of the scholasticism of that time and became more and more absorbed in the study of the Oriental and biblical languages. After entering the Congregation of the Oratory he became acquainted with Jonás Salvador and some other Jewish scholars who introduced him to the rabbinic and Talmudic literature.

As a result of his unique formation Simon began his original scholarly work with an attitude and a method which was remarkably modern for those days. At a time when speculation was the predominant interest, he offered his work as that of a philologist, historian, and critic. Instead of merely citing the theologians as a method of proof, he insisted on going back to the sources, Sacred Scripture and the Fathers of the Church, studying them according to the methods of scientific philology and historiography. He indicates this approach in the prologue of his first important book:

> I have carefully read the works of the principal authors who have written on the criticism of the Bible. . . . I have had at my disposal practically all of the means required for this type of work. I have had at my disposal for a long time many books which were brought from the East and which are at present in the

Paris library of the Oratorian Fathers. I have medi-
tated for a long time on a work of such importance.
With the help of my friends I have consulted many
learned and intelligent men. But after all this consulta-
tion I have discovered that until now no one has really
probed into the core of scriptural criticism. Each one
has treated it, for the most part, according to his own
prejudices. The Jews . . . who only consult their own
authors . . . The Fathers of the Church . . . entirely
neglected the Hebrew text. . . . The two Buxtorfs . . .
have shown . . . only an infatuation for the opinions of
the rabbis, without having consulted other authors.
. . . Father Morin, on the contrary, has an obsession
against the rabbis, without having read them. . . . Cappelli shows more discretion in his criticism . . . but he
has too many variant readings. . . . Voss has tried to
defend the Septuagint translation, but only under the
pretext of rejecting the Masoretic text.[5] . . . There are
few persons who are capable of preserving the balance
which is needed for the discovery of truth. For this
reason I have tried in this book, as far as possible, to
keep the authority of the original Hebrew text and its
translations. I have no exclusive preference for Greek
or Latin or Hebrew or any other language, but I have
carefully examined the Hebrew text and all its translations according to the customary rules of criticism.[6]

Though Simon was attacking Spinoza as well as
Protestantism, his attitude was scientific rather than
apologetic. He did not form his theories merely to
refute Spinoza, since he was well aware that the deistic

Jewish scholar had made many sound observations. Rather it was Spinoza's denial of scriptural inspiration which Simon attacked. His method was to try to harmonize the many criticisms of the Bible with the doctrine of the Church wherever this was possible. If the men who condemned Simon had employed a similarly objective method of investigation, perhaps Simon would have had the opportunity to destroy Spinoza's whole theory. Likewise, though Simon did not set out to refute Protestant biblical theory, his scientific methods of research and clear analysis of the problems involved resulted in a conclusion which certainly undermined fundamentalist Protestantism: "The Scripture is not a book of absolute clarity, and is not sufficient without Tradition."

The Protestant theologians quickly and forcefully answered this challenge. First of all the Anglican Bishop De Veil published a letter of refutation in May, 1678. Simon replied two months later. Toward the end of that year the Protestant theologian, Friedrich Spanheim II published a brief tract praising Simon, but also attempting to refute his conclusions. Since Spanheim's tract was rather superficial, Simon was able to answer his objections only a short time afterward. The criticisms of the Windsor Canon, Isaac Voss, were even less substantial, but were expressed in a violent, polemical style. Voss and Simon's other adversaries accused him of Spinozism, though it was Simon himself who had actually outlined the method of refuting the deistic philosopher.

The Protestant theologians, however, were not the only ones who opposed Simon's critical work. He did indeed exaggerate and fall into occasional errors, but this was no justification for the harsh treatment accorded him by Bishop Jacques-Bénigne Bossuet and other Catholic authorities. The *Disquisitiones biblicae*, published in 1682 by the Franciscan biblical scholar, Claude Frassen, typifies the Catholic reaction against Simon. For example, the Pentateuch, which tradition has attributed to Moses, closes its last book (Deuteronomy) with a description of Moses' death. It had already occurred to many scholars that Moses did not narrate his own death before dying, though a few did defend the thesis that God had revealed to Moses the manner of his death so that he could describe it for the purposes of subsequent history. Flavius Josephus, the Greek-writing historian of the Jews, A.D. 37–95, held this theory. El Tostado (a professor at Salamanca who translated the entire Bible into Valencian in 1478) maintained that the last verses of Deuteronomy were not authored by Moses, and other Catholic scholars followed this interpretation. But Frassen did not like this solution. Here is his argument: "But this solution favors our opponents too much" (*At haec solutio . . . nimium favet Adversariis*). In other words, he is not interested in the truth so much as the refutation of his adversaries. His general approach is also evident when he attempts to answer a difficulty arising from certain geographical references which are anachronistic. He argues as follows: "But this answer concedes too much to our adversaries, and it also tends to favor the opinions of those who claim that Moses wrote none of the Pentateuch. For thus the way is prepared for thinking that not only the words but even entire sentences and extraneous narrations . . . were inserted by Esdras."

Frassen caps his critical estimate with an eloquent appeal: "You see, then, Catholic Reader, into what frightening depths of error those men fall who desire too much knowledge, once they have cast aside the simplicity of faith, and rejected the traditions of our ancestors. But, since all their theories are vain and groundless, the product of men who waste their leisure time, we can reject them with little effort, just as they were proposed without good reason."[7] Frassen sincerely believed that he could undertake the defense of Catholicism and the Bible with arguments such as the ones just quoted!

Bossuet's methods of attacking Simon were not as outlandish as those of Frassen, but he was much more effective.[8] Since he could not attack Simon on the grounds of bad scholarship, Bossuet aroused suspicions against the Oratorian priest on the basis of his occasional rashness. It is not to Bossuet's credit that he employed the full weight of his authority and influence in court to destroy Simon's work.

In short, a fruitful avenue of study was temporarily lost to Catholic biblical scholarship because of the exaggerated zeal of the conservative element in the Church. At the same time, the methods discovered by Simon were left at the disposal of the new Rationalist school. If Simon had been allowed free scope for his research, Catholic biblical scholarship would almost certainly have made great forward strides, unchecked by opposition from the Rationalist school.

## TEXTUAL CRITICISM

The critical method which Simon used was primarily of the literary and historical type. But Louis Cappelli, a Protestant scholar whom Simon singled out for praise, was employing the methods of *textual* criticism at a time when a good many "orthodox" Protestants taught that God had dictated the entire Bible, words, accents, punctuation marks, and all. This "orthodox" theory, however, is very difficult to defend.

As an example we might take a passage from Isaiah, dating from the eighth century B.C. The original text is the only one which is inspired, though it can be transmitted through any number of genuine copies.

But any translation whatever, no matter how faithful it is to the original text, cannot *by itself* be said to be inspired. At best it is merely an excellent translation of an inspired text. The biblical scholar is very interested, obviously, in establishing the original and only inspired text. But many extremely important changes have occurred during the 27 centuries which separate the present from the eighth century B.C.: a different way of pronouncing the Hebrew language, a new way of writing the alphabet (the "square" script), historical and phonetic adaptations in transmitting the text, changes in vocabulary and syntax, the continual copying of original texts by authorized scribes, the exile and dispersion of the Jewish people, the loss of the original metrical tradition, the Jewish rejection of Christianity, the Middle Ages, and many other historical developments. Now with all these developments as a background, how can anyone be certain when he reads the song of Isaiah in the present-day text that he is in contact with the very words which were originally inspired by God? Though it is true that God's providence takes care of the birds and the flowers by natural means, we cannot conclude that this providence also miraculously extends to the smallest accents of the inspired book or to words which could hardly have been written in the prophet's own time. God's providence may indeed be very special, but that does not make it miraculous. Rather, God's providence has taken care that the inspired books be preserved in their substance, allowing at the same time a few errors to creep in as the text was transmitted from generation to generation.

Only a science such as "textual criticism" can account for these errors of transmission. This technique has now been developed into a carefully established set of norms and methods. In the first place the textual critics have determined the different ways in which a copyist might change the original text either deliberately or accidentally (visual, audial, and intentional errors). Secondly, these critics reconstruct the textual families of the copies by which the original was transmitted. But these are only the preparatory tools. For since textual criticism is a fine art, the critic must also examine and try to determine in each case the origin of any error. In doing this, he must be as shrewd as a detective.

Here is a rather involved example of a problem in textual criticism. In St. Paul's First Letter to the Corinthians, Chapter IV, Verse 6, we come upon a confusing sentence: "I have applied these things to myself . . . by way of illustration . . . that . . . you may learn not to be puffed up . . . transgressing what is written." The biblical commentators cannot agree in explaining this sentence and many conjecture that the text was poorly transmitted. In detective-story fashion, they suspect a slight "crime" against the text, a crime of which only vague clues remain. Here is an analysis of the "crime" given by one of the textual "detectives": the sentence should be emended because not all of it belongs in the text. He reconstructed the "crime" in the following manner:

The present text reads:

*ἵνα ἐν ἡμῖν μάθητε*

that in our case you may learn

*τὸ μὴ ὑπὲρ ἃ γέγραπται*

not to know more than what is written

*ἵνα μὴ εἷς ὑπὲρ τοῦ ἑνὸς φυσιοῦσθε*

that no one may be puffed up at another's expense

The original text reads:

*ἵνα μάθητε φρονεῖν*

that you may learn to be prudent

*ἵνα μὴ εἷς ὑπὲρ τοῦ ἑνὸς φυσιοῦσθε*

that no one may be puffed up at another's expense

The scribe neglected to copy the negative, so in his revised text he wrote the negative between the lines:

*ἵνα μάθητε φρονεῖν*

that you may learn to be prudent

*μὴ*

not

*ἵνα εἷς φυσιοῦσθε*

that one may be puffed up . . .

67

The next scribe copied this down correctly, but because he wanted to be perfectly accurate, he noted in the margin that the "not" had been written between the lines and over the letter "a" in the word "that";

ἵνα μάθητε φρονεῖν

that you may learn to be prudent

ἵνα μὴ εἷς . . . φυσιοῦσθε

that no one may be puffed up

(τὸ μὴ ὑπὲρ ἃ γέγραπται)

(the "no" is written over the "a")

The next copyist took the marginal note as a genuine addition and incorporated it into the text. In Greek, however, the letter "a" can be the neutral relative pronoun, meaning "that which." Thus by incorporating the marginal note into the text he effected a change in its meaning:

ἵνα μάθητε

that you may learn

τὸ μὴ ὑπὲρ ἃ γέγραπται φρονεῖν

not to know more than what is written

ἵνα μὴ εἷς ὑπὲρ τοῦ ἑνὸς φυσιοῦσθε

that no one may be puffed up at another's expense

This is the rather ingenious but not altogether certain reconstruction of a textual critic. Most of the problems are less difficult and often the variant readings do not alter the meaning. At other times the correction is obvious. In view of the many developments which the original texts of the Bible have undergone, the present text is surprisingly intact and close to the original. In some cases even the old sounds of the words have been preserved, though a new method of spelling was adopted. In other cases, such as Ezekiel, the texts have been poorly preserved. But throughout the whole process God's providence has been active in a special, though nonmiraculous, way. He chose the Jewish people for the very purpose of realizing this providential plan.

## THE TRANSMISSION OF THE TEXT

The text of the Old Testament underwent many interesting developments during its transmission. Up until the first century of the Christian era there were many re-edited and widely differing copies of the original text. After the destruction of the Jewish nation in A.D. 135, some Jewish textual experts formed academies for the purpose of preserving and transmitting the sacred text. Uniformity (the elimination of variant readings together with the oral transmission of commentaries on the resultant text) was the primary objective of these academies. But the commentaries kept mounting until they became an impossible burden for the memory, so that eventually (about the sixth century) this oral tradition or Masora was put in writing. The Masoretic scholars also invented a system for transmitting the vowels which had been written down only partially in the old Hebrew script. As a result the text which had become uniform, now became immutable and passed through the Middle Ages without being changed. The oldest copies of the text now in existence can be traced back to the Masoretes of the ninth and tenth centuries, and when the Jewish scholar Jacob ben Hayyim printed the first critical text of the Old Testament at Venice in 1525, he used the Masoretic texts as his source material.

The founder of Hebraic philology was the Egyptian Jew, Saadia al-Fayyumi, who flourished in the early tenth century. His methods, derived from the Arab philologists, spread through Spain, France and almost all of Europe. The learned Catholics studied Hebrew in the rabbinic schools and learned the Hebraic philology which had become traditional for the European Jewish scholars.

During the Counter Reformation, however, the text of the Bible became a subject of controversy. Some Catholic scholars played down the Latin Vulgate translation in favor of the original Hebrew text. Other scholars considered the Hebrew worthless, accusing the Jews of deliberately falsifying the text.

In sixteenth-century Spain, Hebrew schools were

flourishing and were directed for the most part by Jewish teachers. The best known Spanish Hebraic scholars were Benito Arias Montano and Fray Luis de León. Both of them were denounced before the Inquisition for their judaizing tendencies, but were given their freedom after a careful investigation. The motive behind such denunciations was not merely a love for orthodoxy. We can also discern emotional tensions, prejudices, and an overly-strict interpretation of the Council of Trent's decrees regarding the Vulgate translation.

Valbuena tells the story of León de Castro, a man deeply involved in this struggle:

> Castro was a man of great learning, especially in the fields of Greek and Latin. On the other hand, he knew no Hebrew, and was violently anti-Semitic in addition. Nevertheless he wrote many lengthy books which were poorly received. Among them was a commentary on the book of Isaiah. A certain anecdote reveals the strong feelings present in both Castro and Fray Luis de León, though the latter was a man of greater prudence, good humor, and pliability. On this particular occasion Fray Luis told Castro that his commentary on Isaiah would be publicly burned. The enraged Castro replied that the flames would first consume Fray Luis and his *relatives.* This reference and some others which crop up during Fray Luis' trial seem to indicate that his reputed Jewish blood was being dragged into the controversy. The college students of the time then divided

into factions, one of which followed Castro's traditionalist approach, claiming that they belonged "to Jesus Christ's party." Castro kept up his anti-Semitic bias and continued to denounce Fray Luis. His constant attacks embittered Arias Montano, though he was a peaceloving man and a significant figure in the theological developments of his day.

Castro's opposition to Fray Luis might perhaps be explained by his own personal failure as a teacher. A document of the time tells us that Castro's students were very angry at his despotic practices and once went to his house to demand an explanation. But "before they could even retaliate, he beat them right out of his house." Unfortunately, though he was a sincere man at heart, his limited intelligence concealed from him his own bias and stubbornness. In other respects he was a learned man—which is not to say that he was an intelligent man—and was very familiar with Greek and Latin, though not with Hebrew, a fact which may have contributed to the anti-Semitism of his doctrine.[9]

The anti-Semitic scholars of that time, as we saw previously, maintained that the Jews had falsified the original Hebrew text. These scholars felt that they were defending the Vulgate translation and upholding the decrees of the Council of Trent by this argument. Actually they were making a groundless accusation against the very people who had diligently preserved the Hebrew text. Melchior Cano made the same accusation, though his motive was not anti-Semitic bias so much as excessive zeal in defending the

Vulgate. The Anglican Canon, Isaac Voss, used this same attack in his fight against Richard Simon.

Further research into the official interpretations of the decrees of Trent has clearly shown the injustice of these charges. Divine providence itself seems to have taken a hand in justifying the faithful Hebrew scribes, for among the recently discovered Dead Sea scrolls was an entire text of the book of Isaiah. This text bore a very close resemblance to the medieval Masoretic text, although they were separated by almost ten centuries. This was no great surprise to the scholars, yet it remains as a remarkable confirmation of the work of the Masoretes.

## LITERARY CRITICISM

Textual criticism was able to produce two definite results: a real confidence in our present biblical text; and secondly, the means for approximating the original in cases of doubt. We must now indicate the critic's job once the original text has been established.

It is at this point that the *literary* critic steps in. His job is to uncover the literary and even preliterary history of the original text, a work which is necessary if the text is to be interpreted correctly. An art analyst, for example, can easily study the history or prehistory of a painting. Without endangering the picture, a quartz lamp can be used to reveal the development of a painting—both the retouch-jobs and the original itself. The same cannot be done, however, in the case of biblical literature, where painstaking comparisons, checks and rechecks can produce only probable results. And even when these probable results have been achieved, the critic must question the literary and historical elements of the texts themselves and of the sources used by the biblical authors. In sum, the critic's path is almost endless once he has begun his journey.

Richard Simon was primarily responsible for this new interest in literary criticism. Of course the Fathers of the Church and the great biblical commentators employed the methods of literary criticism to some extent. But it was the work of Simon which brought on the use of criticism as a systematic method, though his method encountered great opposition at first.

About a hundred years after Simon, a French Catholic physician named Jean Astruc published the results of his scriptural research in a book entitled, *Conjectures regarding the Sources Which It Seems Moses Used in Composing the Book of Genesis.*[10] Astruc's "conjecture" was based on the occurrence of two different names for the divinity, Elohim and Yahweh, a fact which seemed to indicate the presence of two distinct sources. He also noted that some narratives seemed to appear twice. Astruc then carefully separated the "Elohim passages" from the "Yahweh passages" and came up with two distinct and relatively coherent narrative elements. He had thus solved a host of difficulties arising from the apparent contradictions in the text.

Astruc went on analyzing the sacred books, careful all the while to preserve the literary and historical significance of the texts. Fully aware of the novelty of his theory, he made a considerable delay before deciding to publish his work. Even then, he selected a very modest title (*Conjectures*), omitted his own name, changed the publisher's name, and gave a false place of publication. Whenever his real name appeared in his other books, he was careful to disassociate himself from such authors as Locke or Spinoza. In addition he explicitly opposed the Jansenists and Encyclopedists, a stand which made him the object of many jibes from the lips of men like d'Alembert and Voltaire.

Those who commented on Astruc's book were few and ill-disposed. Most of them felt that the new theory had compromised religion. One of the bitterest opponents thought that the *Conjectures* were false and dangerous, ending his commentary with the piteous outcry: "What a shame for the Church! What an insult to Moses! What an injury to the Holy Spirit!" Many French Catholic authors also feared that their liberal-minded enemies would make capital of the new theory. Paradoxically, Astruc's theory was left at the disposal of Protestantism once it had suffered such harsh criticism from the Catholics who wanted to uphold the Scriptures and religious authority.

Johann Michaelis and Heinrich Scharbau, the first German scholars to comment on Astruc, also offered harsh criticism. Michaelis attacked Astruc's lack of educational background, while Scharbau condemned his critical attitude with the simple judgment, "He is a genuine descendent of Simon." Very soon, however, some Protestants of the Rationalist school, particularly Johann S. Semler and Johann G. Eichhorn, successfully introduced the critical method into scientific biblical research.

Thus the method of literary criticism, though it began in a Catholic environment, grew to maturity in a Rationalist atmosphere. As a result, most Catholics felt that the method, if not openly heretical, was at least dangerous to their faith. With the passage of time the method returned to its origins in Catholicism, but only after it had been divorced from its Rationalist connections.

It should be clear, then, that the method of literary criticism, though it has only been used recently by Catholic scholars, dates back four centuries. Today all Old Testament scholars, Catholic and Protestant alike, employ critical methods. In fact there is hardly any difference between them; for most Protestant scholars have either employed the traditional critical method, which many Catholics accept, or have developed it further. Literary criticism has thus brought about the separation of unacceptable from sound critical principles. In the following chapter I will indicate how this separation occurred and why it took so long to develop.

## The Attack against Critical Method

In addition to the conquest of rationalism over the past fifty years, a new movement against literary criticism took place as a result of some important archaeological discoveries.

Textual and literary criticism began in the scholar's room behind closed doors and after countless hours of scanning the texts. Then quite abruptly, almost as if by some prearranged plan, the scholars emerged into the open air to dig up secrets buried beneath the earth and to reconstruct the past with solid evidence. Thus an abundance of new information was made available to biblical scholars, aiding them to reformulate their theories or compelling them to change their hypotheses. At the same time, the public was informed of these great archaeological discoveries, through for example, Ceram's highly popular book, *Gods, Graves and Scholars*[11] and Keller's even more popular book, already referred to, *The Bible as History*.

Despite the popularity of Keller's book, scholars have had little use for it. The reason for their reservations was not so much the presence of several obvious errors as the false impression it gives to the general public. The subtitle of the book, *Archaeology Confirms the Book of Books*, is at least misleading, if not positively false. The Introduction to the book ends with the following statement: "In view of the overwhelming mass of authentic and well-attested evidence now available, as I thought of the sceptical criticism which from the eighteenth century onwards would fain have demolished the Bible altogether, there kept hammering on my brain this one sentence: "The Bible is right after all!"[12]

The orientation of the entire book as well as the tone of the title and Introduction come down to this: archaeology opposes criticism, which in turn opposes the Bible; archaeology fights on the side of the Bible; criticism is defeated while archaeology emerges victorious. No doubt much authentic data is well presented and reasonably explained in the course of the book's 400 pages. But the evidence presented often suffers from the questionable theory on which it rests.

One brief chapter, for example, is entitled, "Digging up the Flood." We read toward the end of this chapter that "A vast catastrophic inundation, resembling the Biblical Flood which had regularly been described by sceptics as either a fairy tale or a legend, had not only taken place but was moreover an event within the compass of history. . . . It happened about 4000 B.C."[13] Keller derived his facts from information published by the excavator, Sir Leonard Woolley. But he neglected to mention the fact that Woolley himself retracted his original conclusions as a result of further soundings. The layer of mud which had previously been taken as evidence of a flood did not cover the hill completely. Hence it was probably not the effect of a flood, but rather the deposit from a body of water which almost covered the entire hill for many centuries. Keller seems to have ignored or else deliberately omitted this modification in Woolley's theory.

Further, while discussing the walls of Jericho, Keller failed to mention the contradictory and inconclusive evidence which the excavators found. All he did was to make a reference to Miss Kathleen Kenyon's excavations on prebiblical levels. But he left the reader with the same impression that John Garstang entertained several years before, namely that the walls had been ruined by an earthquake, that there was evidence of a destruction by fire and that this had occurred during Joshua's time. No archaeologist today would agree with Keller's reconstruction because Miss Kenyon's discoveries on the biblical levels have been continually revised and have practically disproved the theories first proposed by Garstang.

Keller's chapter on Jericho concludes with a vague

reference which can easily leave a false impression in the reader's mind. After referring to the rite of circumcision which was performed at Gilgal with stone knives, Keller adds: "Ten miles northwest of Bethel lies Kefr Ish'a, the 'Village of Joshua.' In the neighbouring hillside are some rock tombs. In 1870 in one of these sepulchres a number of stone knives was found . . ."[14] The reader, if he is taken in by the style of the book, would naturally tend to accept this fact as a clear proof. But if the reader happens to know that the hill in question is twenty-five miles from Gilgal and that in 1870 the precise labeling and assessment of the discoveries had not yet been done, he will look upon the fact as an interesting but inconclusive piece of evidence.

Such is the method of Keller's book and this is the way he defends the historicity of the Bible. What will happen when the open-minded reader discovers the many inprecisions of the book? Perhaps he will draw the conclusion that the Bible is inaccurate after all. We can be grateful that archaeology has rendered us a more positive service than that of the talented journalist. But we can at least give him the credit for having stimulated the public's interest and for revealing much significant and well-grounded information.

Keller's book also has the virtue of reflecting on the popular level the situation which obtained among scholars about thirty or forty years ago. We already saw how Keller in his Introduction expressed the opposition between criticism and archaeology. Today this opposition no longer exists. For example the great archaeologist of Palestine, William F. Albright, has used critical method to great advantage. In fact any student of the biblical sciences today will employ critical as well as archaeological method. But forty years ago there was little basis for agreement between the two methods since criticism relied exclusively on philosophy and comparative religion while archaeology was based on historical and tangible evidence.

The literary critic at that time was a prisoner of his biblical text. He brought his philosophical and religious ideas into this self-made intellectual prison. Among these ideas was the radical denial of the supernaturality of the Bible. Due to these self-imposed limitations, critics developed a deep distrust in the historical value of the deeds narrated by the Old Testament writers. The critics traced most of the narratives back to previous documents, which in turn they traced back to the creative imagination of the original writer.

The archaeologists, searching for facts and independent data, broke through these arbitrary critical limitations. Fifty years ago the more bellicose archaeologists had for their slogan "criticize the critics." The library scholars were bent on maintaining their own theories and played down the discoveries of the pick-and-shovel scholars. On their side, the archaeologists were digging up data which was a threat to many of the critics' theories. The new generation of scholars fought with a very effective weapon, for a single swing of the pick could make any merely theoretical edifice crumble.

Take the art of writing, for example. The traditional theory was that in Moses' time the art of writing was unknown in Canaan. But the discovery of a letter or tablet which could be dated with certainty was enough to destroy the entire theory, all the more so since the excavations revealed five different types of writing used at that time. There was also a presumption that Israel lived in a state of isolation from its environment and had no transactions with the neighboring cities. But this theory became improbable and arbitrary after the discovery of an archive of letters dated from the fourteenth century B.C. These letters reflected an active epistolary interchange in a tongue admitted to be a *lingua franca* for international relationships.

Some critics, feeling uneasy about their position, sought a compromise by granting the facts unearthed by archaeologists, and then claiming that they agreed with their own theories. This exemplifies the "concordistic" attitude already mentioned. These critics conceded that a known fact was more valuable than a brilliant hypothesis, but they added that the facts were in marvelous accord with their own hypotheses. Such a compromise, however, could never achieve lasting success, since the archaeological discoveries required that many of the critics' theories be drastically revised.

Fifty years ago Melvin Grove Kyle explained this situation with abundant evidence and a moderate tone.[15] The title of his book, *The Deciding Voice of the Monuments in Biblical Criticism,* indicates the decisive competence which archaeological facts have, while the book's contents demonstrate the value of archaeology in giving us a general framework for the biblical narratives. He also points out the importance of achaeology as a basis for good critical method, since it provides an abundance of evidence which the critic can use to prove his theories.

Such was the situation fifty years ago. Catholic scholars were overjoyed at this change in orientation since it discredited radicalism and seemed to confirm the more traditional theories. Between the two world wars the golden age of Palestinian archaeology moved along at a regular pace, with a sensational discovery here and there. The Lachish letters, for example, awakened widespread interest. These letters were written in ink on potsherds at a time of military crisis.[16] Of even greater importance was the discovery of a library written in a simplified cuneiform script and in a previously unknown language (Ugaritic) which was soon identified as similar to the ancient Hebrew.

During this interbellum period, therefore, an entire change of attitude occurred. The year 1930 might be singled out as the point at which this change became evident. The new attitude grew and established itself more firmly during the 30s, though there were no spectacular discoveries. Then came the enforced silence occasioned by World War II, during which Pius XII stated the new policy which is contained in his encyclical, *Divino afflante Spiritu*. When the war ended, circumstances demanded a renewal of study and a meeting of scholars. Since attitudes had quietly matured in the interim, this meeting was made easier and the public's interest grew with surprising speed.

## Cooperation with Criticism

Now that the polemic and its underlying causes have passed away, archaeology works together with criticism in a peaceful manner. In his recent book, *Biblical Archaeology*, G. Ernest Wright accurately describes the work of archaeology:

> The biblical archaeologist may or may not be an excavator himself, but he studies the discoveries of the excavations in order to glean from them every fact that throws a direct, indirect or even diffused light upon the Bible. . . . Yet his chief concern is not with methods or pots or weapons in themselves alone. His central and absorbing interest is the understanding and exposition of the Scriptures . . .
>
> Biblical man, unlike other men in the world, had learned to confess his faith by telling the story of what

had happened to his people and by seeing within it the hand of God. Faith was communicated, in other words, through the forms of history, and unless history is taken seriously one cannot comprehend biblical faith which triumphantly affirms the meaning of history. . . . archaeology is his aid in recovering the nature of a period long past . . .

Biblical man could express his faith so confidently because he understood that the events he describes really happened. If we are to take him seriously, we must also take his history seriously; and the more we know about it, the more we shall be enlightened by what he says concerning it. The intensive study of the biblical archaeologist is thus the fruit of the vital concern for history which the Bible has instilled in us. We cannot, therefore, assume that the knowledge of biblical history is unessential to the faith. Biblical theology and biblical archaeology must go hand in hand, if we are to comprehend the Bible's meaning . . .

For the most part archaeology has substantiated and illumined the biblical story at so many crucial points that no one can seriously say that it is little but a congeries of myth and legend. . . . Yet numerous historical problems have arisen, as we shall see in the pages which follow, and in addition there is in the Bible an interpretation of events and of experience which is not subject to historical or archaeological testing. That a violent wave of destruction occurred in southern Palestine during the course of the 13th century B.C. is clear from the excavations. That this was caused by the Israelite invasion is a reasonable historical inference. That the warfare was directed by God for his own righteous ends in history is, however, an interpretation by faith which is not subject to historical testing.[17]

Here we have an explanation which is characteristically modern and constructive. It is the sort of attitude which should stimulate anyone who is seriously interested in the Bible. We see here, in addition to the writer's faith, which we can take for granted, a confidence in the Bible as a historical document, a serenity when faced with critical analysis, and a sobriety in the presentation of evidence. But we do not detect the apologetic attitude which tries to prove everything, nor the systematic abhorrence of any kind of criticism, nor finally any flippancy in treating a subject as serious as the Sacred Scriptures.

Another quotation from Wright's book reflects his attitude toward modern biblical studies:

> In this perspective the biblical scholar no longer bothers to ask whether archaeology "proves" the Bible. In the sense that the biblical languages, the life and customs of its peoples, its history, and its conceptions are illuminated in innumerable ways by the archaeological discoveries, he knows that such a question is certainly to be answered in the affirmative. . . . the scholar also knows that the primary purpose of biblical archaeology is not to "prove" but to discover. The vast majority of the "finds" neither prove nor disprove; they fill in the background and give the setting for the story. It is unfortunate that this desire to "prove" the Bible has vitiated so many works which

are available to the average reader. The evidence has been misused, and the inferences drawn from it are often misleading, mistaken, or half true. Our ultimate aim must not be "proof," but truth.[18]

We can fittingly conclude this chapter with Pope Pius XII's words on this subject in his encyclical of 1943:

> . . . [in the times of Leo XIII] hardly a single place in Palestine had begun to be explored by means of relevant excavations. Now, however, this kind of investigation is much more frequent and, since more precise methods and technical skills have been developed as a result of actual experience, it gives us information at once more abundant and more accurate. How much light has been derived from these explorations for the more correct and fuller understanding of the Sacred Books all experts know, as well as all those who devote themselves to these studies. The value of these excavations is enhanced by the discovery from time to time of written documents which help a great deal toward the knowledge of the languages, letters, events, customs and forms of worship of very ancient times.[19]

# Chapter III.
# Literary Problems

Now that the work of archaeology has made such progress and confidence has been restored in the Bible, the scholars are going back to the text itself. Of course the text had not been entirely overlooked while archaeology was having its heyday in the interbellum period. Nor would anyone say that archaeology has been abandoned today, though the dominant interest lies elsewhere. Contemporary circumstances do not particularly favor archaeological investigation, whereas the text attracts the scholar because of its new problems.

The most important excavations in recent years have been carried out by the Israeli at Hazor, by Americans at Gibeon and Balata (ancient Shechem), by the English at Tell es-Sultan (Old Testament Jericho), and by the École biblique at Qumran and Tell el-Far'ah. The scrolls discovered in the caves near the Dead Sea, on the other hand, have captured the interest of a large number of research specialists. Lastly, a good portion of the material available for archaeological investigation in other places has yet to be examined and adequately assessed. There is, consequently, a definite centering of interest today on the text of the Bible rather than on its archaeological framework.

Now that we approach the Bible with a changed attitude, it reveals many new insights to us. But the problems connected with these insights have been just as numerous. It almost seems to be a part of the Bible's destiny to supply students with an unending source of new probelms and labors. Pius XII discusses this problem in his encyclical:

> Nevertheless, no one should be surprised that all difficulties have not yet been solved and overcome; and that even today serious problems greatly challenge the minds of Catholic exegetes. We should not lose courage on this account; nor should we forget that in the human sciences the same happens as in the natural world; that is to say, new beginnings grow little by little and fruits are gathered only after many labors. Thus it has happened that certain disputed points, which in the past remained unsolved and in suspense, in our days, with the progress of studies, have found a satisfactory solution. Hence there are grounds for hoping that those problems which now seem most involved and difficult will, through constant effort, at last be clarified.
>
> And if the wished-for solution is slow in coming or does not satisfy us, since perhaps a successful conclusion may be reserved to posterity, let us not therefore become impatient, since we find verified in ourselves what the Fathers, and especially Augustine, observed

in their own time, namely that God wished difficulties to be scattered throughout the Sacred Books inspired by Him in order that we might be urged to read and scrutinize them more intently, and thus experiencing in a salutary manner our own limitations, we might be exercised in due submission of mind. It is no wonder if no wholly satisfactory solution to one or another question will ever be found, since sometimes we are dealing with matters obscure in themselves and too remote from our times and our experience; and since exegesis also, like any other important science, has its secrets, which, impenetrable to our minds, can be solved by no effort whatever.[1]

### RECENT DIFFICULTIES

The problems created by our new insights into the Bible's meaning have been the source of the scandal or surprise mentioned at the beginning of this book. At the very moment when we would hope that men's minds are at peace, we discover instead an antagonism born of misunderstanding. The result is suspicion and sometimes open attack against modern biblical criticism.

Here is an example to illustrate this attitude. In a certain suburb of Havana, the annual feast of St. Lazarus is very popular. Multitudes of devoted followers gather together at this time for the solemn procession in the "Saint's" honor. But one year their bishop, thinking that such a devotion was an abuse, wanted to suppress the custom. It was indeed an abuse; for the St. Lazarus being honored was not the Lazarus of Bethany, the brother of Martha and Mary, but the beggar Lazarus who wanted the crumbs from the rich man's table. The townspeople resisted their bishop because they felt that it would be seriously wrong for them to abandon their saint who, according to the testimony of Jesus Christ Himself, was brought by the angels to Abraham's bosom. The rights of the case, at least regarding the point at issue, were clearly on the bishop's side; for the townspeople had based their argument on a false assumption. They had understood as history what was, in reality, only a parable.

Here we see all the elements of the modern problem. A group in a Christian town, including some priests educated in a different age, put up a protest because the Scripture scholars had denied the historicity of figures or facts which they had understood as pure history.

The biblical scholar frequently hears the complaint that soon there will be nothing left of the original Bible. He can only answer that it will all be left, save for some marginal glosses and errors. The Catholic scholar professes, after all, that the entire Bible, just as the Catholic Church teaches and according to the norms laid down by the Council of Trent, is inspired by God and hence is the word of God. Thus the entire

Bible will remain; for the critic does not want to dissect but rather to interpret it.

Another complaint is that if the historicity of *this* passage is denied, it will become impossible to guarantee the historicity of the remainder. The biblical scholar replies by distinguishing; for to criticize means to separate. One must realize, first of all, that it is incorrect to look upon the Old Testament as a ponderous history comprised of so many volumes or books. The Old Testament is an almost completely heterogeneous work of literature. Besides the general framework of history, it contains such diversified material as sermons, poems, proverbs, psalms, prophecies, fables, laws, and so forth. Most Catholic exegetes today are not trying to play down the value of any part of the Bible but rather to look for a proper division into categories which will do greater justice to the content and literary type of the diverse elements. For generations the traditional categories have been handed down, but the time has now come for a critical revision of these categories. If the work is done with moderation and reverence, the reader will profit from it, since any piece of literature can be better appreciated when it is placed in its proper literary genre. The work of the modern critic may appear to be rather novel, but the reflective reader will realize that the only novel element is the systematic breadth of scope with which the work is now being approached.

## THE PROBLEM OF LITERARY OBJECTIVITY

There are two hidden assumptions which are at the root of the objections previously mentioned. The first assumption consists in a rather naïve concept of literary objectivity, while the second demands the exclusivist definition of the strictly historical. It should prove helpful to analyze the roots of these two assumptions.

To begin with, any explanation in terms of language necessarily involves a transformation of reality. Reality and our experience of it are stylized and expressed through the medium of language. Thus reality and experience are not *de*formed, but rather *con*formed through language. Language is a power which teaches us to understand and to order the world as well as to shape our own experiences.[2] The great writers, while enriching the instrumentality of language, have likewise enriched our capacity for ordered perception. For the most part, therefore, the naïve realism of language can no longer be maintained.

The external world confronts man and longs to be discovered. When man perceives this world, he humanizes it. This does not mean that man deforms or falsifies the world, but that their mutual relationship is actuated in a moment of plenitude, since knowing is the perfection of man and being known is the perfection of the external universe. The dawn which a man contemplates in a moment of sorrow is not the same dawn which is seen by a cow when it bellows toward the sky. Nor is the moon of which the romantic poet sings the same as the moon which prompts the dogs to bark during the night. Thus the world is humanized by our living encounters with it, and all the more so according to the intensity which we bring to this experience.

These living experiences, however, possess a quality of totality or completeness and are presented to us as a formless or only half-formed continuum. It is the specific function of language to convert this continuum into discrete parts by applying a system of vocabulary, morphology, and syntax. In this way the experience is given a new and human form. This is the second stage of transformation or interpretation. It does not deform the things of the external universe, but rather gives them a human dimension.

Further, the linguistic form by which I order my experience also has a social function, namely to communicate my interior life to other men, and thus to bring about a strictly personal encounter which is altogether superior to the mere knowledge of objects. This social and interpersonal orientation of language is an additional interpretative factor, one which raises language to all the grandeur of the human.

In the Garden of Paradise, man alone was able to give names to the animals. By doing this, he brought the human order into existence, an order over which he was lord and master. In this he resembled God, who went about giving names to His creatures, thus calling them into existence. Just as man is created in the image and likeness of God, so he creates the world of language according to his own image and likeness.

The field of journalism offers a good example of this. If two newspaper reporters give an account of some occurrence, they will normally include much more material presented in the words of the reporters than one would expect in a purely objective narrative. This is because we usually attempt to reproduce with greater accuracy an experience which is already embodied in the form of language. But the balance of the experience can only receive the form of language through the activity of some narrator.

All language, in fact, consists in a transformation. The occurrences of the past come down to us transformed into linguistic terms, possessing a new, intermediate reality which faithfully, though inadequately, represents the objective reality. One must have this fundamental aspect of language as his point of departure if he is to go on in his study to the forms of literary language. This point is brought out in *Divino afflante Spiritu:* ". . . as, with his customary wisdom, the Angelic Doctor already observed in these words: 'In Scripture Divine things are presented to us in the manner which is in common use amongst men.' For, as the substantial Word of God became like to men in all things, 'except sin,' so the words of God, expressed in human language, are made like to human speech in every respect, except error."[3]

In literary language there is also another type of common transformation which can affect a word or group of words—the metaphor, the image, and the allegory. Not only is reality or experience transformed through linguistic expression, but even language itself can undergo a transformation.

The first exegetes of the early Church felt that the metaphorical or transposed sense of a text had nothing to do with the literal sense. St. Jerome made the important contribution of extending the scope of the literal sense even to the metaphorical sense. In this way the applicability of the literal sense was broadened and a more sober and objective interpretation of the sacred text became possible. If the Israelite poet calls his God "rock," then God is, in the literal sense of the word, "rock" (underscoring the aspect of durability, firmness, and protectiveness). A parable is an integral transposition of a thing into a fictional narrative. The literal sense of the parable is its underlying point. Thus the first task of the reader and commentator is to understand each passage of the Scripture in its literal sense. This is the only firm ground from which the leap to other meanings can be safely effected.

## THE LITERARY FORM
## AND ITS INFLUENCE ON THE WORK

There does exist, however, a type of literary transformation which can affect a work or its context at a
deeper level, namely, the literary form. We might use
for an example some intense religious experience, a
deeply felt appreciation of some providential marvel
wrought by God. Every aspect of both the reality
and the experience tend to be based on this intense
spiritual enthusiasm. If one desires to give literary expression to such an experience, he will naturally select
a unifying form to give order and expansion to the diverse elements involved. One could select the hymnic
form, which is certainly well suited to intense spiritual
feeling. Perhaps the one experiencing such a feeling
will spontaneously choose the hymnic form without
even reflecting on his choice. In any case, this choice
of a literary form has a radical effect on the entire
work of literature, since any expression is meaningful
only when it is referred to the center of interest which
stimulated and sustained it. The very structure of a
poem is articulated in view of its center of focus. Thus
the literary form is an element which affects the entire literary work with all its parts. Since this is true,
no work of literature can be understood correctly
unless it is put into its proper literary focus.

This point can be illustrated by the senses of seeing

and hearing. Even an Academy Award winning film, for example, will be radically deformed if the movie-projector happens to be out of focus. If the focusing apparatus is turned only a couple of degrees, the whole picture will be badly distorted. When the operator of the projector corrects the focus, his only motive is to proportion the picture to normal human vision. There is another type of distortion which can be foisted on the public, such as treating seriously what is in reality only a joke, or treating as real what is actually a mere fantasy. Such distortions are more intellectual and hence more difficult to correct.

Beethoven's *Fifth Symphony* will serve as our second example. The third movement of this work comes to an end with a slow passage where the note is sustained in order to maintain the tonality. Meanwhile, the melody repeats a theme in different tones and intervals in search of a resolution. According to the composer's directions, the fourth movement evolves out of the third movement without any interval, thus resolving the painstaking search through some extraordinarily triumphant and luminous measures—in C-Major and in two fourths time. But let us suppose that the orchestra, once it has reached the fourth movement, maintains the three flats of the preceding and plays in three quarter time. The notes are practically the same and the orchestration does not vary, yet the entire meaning of the finale would be radically deformed due to a simple change of time and a couple of flats. But it is precisely these numbers and flats which give us the "key" to the entire piece of music. If the conductor were to go back to the proper key, he would not be trying to avoid dissonances so much as to give the artistic work its true meaning.

Similarly, if we are to understand a work of literature, we must put it in its proper focus and tonality. Should we fail to do this, our total understanding will be deformed, even though we may understand many of the individual elements. If we cannot discover the proper key and tone, we will certainly produce many dissonances never intended by the original author.

All this holds true, likewise, in the field of biblical studies. When the modern Catholic exegete attempts to determine the literary form of a given book or chapter in the Bible, he is only trying to understand the biblical text in its proper framework. It is true, of course, that the search for literary forms began fifty years ago in an effort to extricate biblical inerrancy from certain difficulties.[4] The people whose attitudes have not changed since those days will think perhaps that the modern exegete is only resorting to the same subterfuge, while the heart of the problem is left untouched. Oddly enough, the modern theory of literary forms bears a close resemblance to Gunkel's Protestant school of biblical interpretation, perhaps because it is the exact opposite. In fact, as Gunkel himself said, a swing to the right is the same as a swing to the left, except that it is in the opposite direction.

Since Gunkel did not believe in the supernatural inspiration of the Bible, he interpreted it merely as another document in the history of religion and literature. It was his opinion that the ancient writers intruded their own personalities into their works very little and readily accepted pre-established forms and canons. Hence it became extremely important for the interpretation of the biblical texts to determine these canons or literary types with precision. The Catholic scholar, on the other hand, believing that the Bible is a supernatural message from God and is communicated through the mediation of the scriptural writers, attempts to determine these forms and canons so that he can reach the authentic divine message. Since Gunkel's methods are still useful on the strictly scientific level, it is easy to understand why the conservative reader might think that the modern Catholic exegete has become a kind of Rationalist after the school of Gunkel. In a similar fashion, Simon was accused of Spinozism because he accepted a few tenets of Spinoza.

Now that the encyclical, *Divino afflante Spiritu*, has been promulgated, however, this charge can no longer be leveled at the modern Catholic biblical scholar. This is evident from the following quotation:

The literal sense of a passage is not always as obvious in the speeches and writings of the ancient authors of the East as it is in the works of the writers of our own time. For what they wished to express is not to be determined by the rules of grammar and philology alone, nor solely by the context; the interpreter must, as it were, go back in spirit to those remote centuries of the East and with the aid of history, archaeology, ethnology and other sciences, accurately determine what modes of writing the authors of that ancient period would be likely to use, and in fact did use.

For the ancient peoples of the East, in order to express their ideas, did not always employ those forms or kinds of speech which we use today; but rather those used by the men of their own times and countries. What those exactly were the commentator cannot determine in advance, but only after a careful examination of the ancient literature of the East. . . .

Hence the Catholic commentator, in order to comply with the present needs of biblical studies, in explaining the Sacred Scripture and in demonstrating and proving its immunity from all error, should also make a prudent use of this means, and should determine, therefore, to what extent the manner of expression or the literary mode adopted by the sacred writer may lead to a correct and genuine interpretation. And let him be convinced that this part of his office cannot be neglected without serious detriment to Catholic exegesis.[5]

Thus the pope expressly tells us that in order to know the real meaning, the literal sense, it is necessary among other things to determine the literary form. The primary objective of sound exegesis is to determine the meaning rather than to solve difficulties. In general, once the authentic key has been established, many of the dissonances automatically disappear:

> Not infrequently—to mention only one instance—when some persons reproachfully charge the Sacred Writers with some historical error or inaccuracy in the recording of facts, it turns out on closer examination to be nothing else than a question of those customary modes of expression and narration peculiar to the ancients, which they employed in the mutual dealings of social life and which were sanctioned by common usage.
>
> When, therefore, such modes of expression are encountered in the sacred text, which, being meant for men, is couched in human language, justice demands that they be no more taxed with error than when they occur in the ordinary intercourse of daily life. By this knowledge and exact appreciation of the modes of speaking and writing in use among the ancients many difficulties can be solved which are raised against the veracity and historical value of the Divine Scriptures; and this study also makes a fruitful contribution to the fuller and more luminous understanding of the mind of the Sacred Writer.[6]

In conclusion we may say that archaeology has solved many problems while it has raised others. But no serious scholar will abandon his work simply because there are many difficult problems confronting him. Likewise it is not the scholar's job to eliminate all difficulties connected with the Bible, for this would be an impossible task. But when the Catholic exegete is interpreting the Bible for the general public, he would do well to concentrate on the positive and constructive rather than the problematic elements.

## THE PROBLEM OF HISTORICITY IN GENERAL

Perhaps the most important of the difficulties confronting the new exegetical orientation is the problem of historicity. Certain books and chapters of the Bible which had previously been read as pure history are now placed in the category of fiction, though they may have *some* historical basis. Fiction, of course, is not the same as falsehood, nor is it an inferior literary category. The parable of the Prodigal Son, for example, is a beautiful fictional narrative in which Christ describes for us the fatherly love of God for men. In Second Samuel, chapters XI and XII, on the other hand, the sacred author recounts for us David's sin and his sincere repentance: "David said to Nathan: I have sinned against the Lord. And Nathan said to David: the Lord has taken away your sin." It would be difficult to maintain that one of these accounts has more truth than the other. In the category of historicity, David's story is no doubt superior, but is true history the only and most profound truth? The story of David tells us a concrete fact, limited by space and time. When it is incorporated into the biblical narrative, it acquires an even greater value. But due to its fictional character, the Gospel parable is not limited to any particular time or place, and reveals to us an eternal and abiding attitude of God toward mankind.

This strange attitude of distrust for the merely literary may possibly be a relic of nineteenth-century Positivism which exalted pure historical objectivity and downgraded the category of literature to that of mere diversion or an impoverished concept of art for art's sake. No one nowadays would deny that Dostoyevski's novels contain a rich fund of human and religious truth and have had a pronounced influence on the modern mind. There is abundant literature for leisure reading, such as detective stories, science-fiction and light romances. But there is also a literature filled with social and religious import. In the same vein, there are movies made for leisure and entertainment, just as there are movies made with an intense human and religious preoccupation. Pope Pius XII often spoke of these different types of movies in his frequent allocutions on the subject.

Thus if a Catholic commentator, such as J. Schildenberger, O.S.B., says that the book of Esther contains a freely developed historical nucleus, he is not saying that the inspired book is mere "escape" literature, but that the religious message of the book is conceived in terms of an imaginative story.[7]

We cannot, however, go to the other extreme and equate history with imaginative fiction, or refuse to discuss the problem of the Bible's historicity in general. The exodus from Egypt, the covenant at Sinai, the occupation of the Promised Land, the election of David, and so forth, are genuine historical facts, masterpieces of the great history of salvation wrought by God in order to save all mankind. Similarly the incarnation, death, and resurrection of Christ, as well as His teaching and miracles, are part of God's great plan of salvation and historically fixed. We should not confuse the historicity of Job with that of David, nor should we put on the same level of historical objectivity the book of Judith and the Gospel narrative of Christ's passion. To criticize means to discriminate, to separate, to assign to each matter its proper place. Hence it would be as false to claim the same degree of historicity for the entire body of Sacred Scripture from Genesis to the Apocalypse as it would be to deny or call in question the historicity of the whole biblical narrative in its every aspect.

Several paragraphs from the encyclical *Humani generis* are relevant to our discussion at this point. Once the pope has censured in it those who either deny, or rather arbitrarily restrict, biblical historicity, the subject is narrowed down to the first chapters of Genesis.

The temptation, the fall, the promises, and so forth, are declared to be real occurrences which happened at some determined moment. For this reason the text which transmits these events to us can and should be designated as "history." But this requires some precision, since the literary form "history" can be subdivided into lower types. There is the Greek way of writing history (Herodotus, Thucydides), the Roman way (Livy, Tacitus), and the nineteenth-century way, with all its critical rigor (Mommsen, von Ranke). The first chapters of Genesis do not pertain to any of these historical methodologies. To what form, then, do they belong? The encyclical does not decide this question, but leaves it up to the biblical commentators: "This letter, in fact, clearly points out that the first eleven chapters of Genesis, although, properly speaking, they do not conform to the historical method used by the best Greek and Latin writers or by competent authors in our time, nevertheless do pertain to history in the true sense, though this must be further studied and determined by exegetes."[8]

Hence the refusal to accept anything which is not purely historical is as erroneous as prescinding entirely from any historical validity. If the second position is radical, then the first is naïve. And just as the Catholic scholar will not encourage radicalism, neither will he recommend naïveté as a scientific or educational ideal. A naïve simplicity might be allowed before the critical question has been raised; but once this is no longer true, the method of serious critical analysis must be employed.

A CONCRETE PROBLEM IN HISTORICITY

In the book of Joshua the conquest and occupation of the Promised Land is narrated in a literary structure and in epic style. It begins with a brief instruction to Joshua from Yahweh:

After Moses, the servant of the Lord, had died, the
  Lord said to Moses' aide, Joshua, son of Nun:
My servant Moses is dead.
So prepare to cross the Jordan here,
  with all the people,
  into the land I will give the Israelites.
As I promised Moses, I will deliver to you
  every place where you set foot. . . .
  from the desert and from Lebanon
  east to the great river Euphrates
  and west to the Great Sea.
No one can withstand you while you live.
I will be with you as I was with Moses:
I will not leave you nor forsake you.
Be firm and steadfast,
  so that you may give this people possession of the land
  which I swore to their fathers I would give them.
Above all, be firm and steadfast,
  taking care to observe the entire Law
  which my servant Moses enjoined on you.

Do not swerve from it either to the right or to the left,
   that you may succeed wherever you go. . . .
I command you: be firm and steadfast!
Do not fear nor be dismayed,
   for the Lord, your God, is with you wherever you go.

It would be possible for us, without any further question, to read this passage as the simple account of God's providential direction of His people in the conquest of the Promised Land through His chosen servant, Joshua. But we could also analyze it according to critical method. Such a critical analysis would reveal the vocabulary, phraseology, stereotyped formulas and stylistic techniques characteristic of a school of hortatory literature developed in an age subsequent to that of Joshua. The very same phrases are found scattered about in other contexts. One author places part of the speech in the mouth of the dying Moses.

We might also ask, while making our critical analysis, whether or not the introduction treats of matter which is strictly historical. If it does, then we would have to say that God somehow spoke to Joshua in the very style which was formulated in the Deuteronomic school. Joshua must then have received the message word-for-word while the author of the book of Joshua later transcribed it either directly or indirectly. To say the least, this explanation seems a bit farfetched and naïve.

We could also attack the problem differently by saying that God directed Joshua, through His special and efficacious providence, to lead the chosen people into the Promised Land. Joshua carried out this plan not in a single action, but rather in a whole series of actions which served as both an end of the escape from Egypt and a fulfillment of the promise made to the patriarchs. God gave His servant the prudence and courage demanded by such a difficult task, a task which God Himself had imposed through the directives given to Moses. God then protected His chosen servant by means of His constant assistance. Such an analysis does justice to both the historical and supernatural facts, though these may be viewed properly only by the enlightened student. In order to drive these facts home to the reader, the biblical author has placed a theological synthesis in God's mouth. Through God's words, then, the author has interpreted for us the true theological significance of the historical fact, inserting the successful outcome of the events into the total miraculous design of the history of salvation.

According to our critical analysis, therefore, the fact of a divine instruction to Joshua in the exact words of the text would not be strictly historical. Nevertheless each one of the words is extremely important if we are to understand correctly the real significance of the historical fact dramatized in the narrative. Even though the critic doubts or considers improbable the strict historicity of the speech, he has not underestimated a single phrase. In fact, it would have been difficult for the sacred writer to find any briefer or more effective means for interpreting the religious fact in narrative terms. Through the mediation of the sacred writer, God, the author of all history, has effectively communicated His ultimate meaning to us.

## THE CHURCH FATHERS
### AND SCRIPTURAL INTERPRETATION

An even more embarrassing question arises at this point; for we must ask how it is that parts of the Bible could have been misunderstood, or at least incorrectly interpreted, for almost twenty centuries. It is like saying that the entire tradition of the Church, from the Church Fathers until today, has been in error. Since this problem involves a transfer from Scripture to Tradition, no facile solution will be found.

In approaching this problem, we must begin by stating that Tradition has always grasped the essential message of Scripture, namely its religious meaning. The scientific discoveries of the past hundred years have added a great deal, however, to the more technical understanding of the Bible. Though the great Renaissance scholar, Arias Montano, is usually recognized as the founder of biblical archaeology, he would suffer by comparison with almost any scholar in the same field today.

We must also keep in mind that the Fathers of the Church had little interest in history. Father Vaccari, in the article cited at the beginning of the book, contrasts modern exegesis with that of antiquity under four different headings: first, the Fathers used translations, whereas the modern scholars base their interpretations on the original text; secondly, the Fathers were particularly interested in the hidden and allegorical meanings, whereas the modern scholar prefers the literal sense; thirdly, the Fathers rarely attempt an organic interpretation of books or entire literary units, whereas the modern scholar will employ both analytic and synthetic methods; lastly, the Fathers had little concern for history, whereas the study of history is one of the predominant interests of the modern scriptural interpreter. It is not surprising therefore that the Fathers failed to produce so much as a single commentary on the historical books of the Old Testament.[9]

In the early centuries of the Church, scholars were only interested in answering the question, "What happened?" or, at best, "How did it happen?" Today, however, the scholar, following von Ranke's tradition, wants an answer to the question, "How did it *really* happen?" (*Wie es eigentlich gewesen?*). Almost the entire attitude of the modern scholar can be summed up in the adverb "really" (*eigentlich*). The Church Fathers never posed this question, so it is useless to ask how they would have answered it.[10]

The modern solution to the historical problem is not quite the same as the traditional solution. This is only to be expected since the problem itself has changed. The new approach is brought out in the letter of the Pontifical Biblical Commission to Cardinal Suhard regarding the date of the sources of the Pentateuch and the literary type of the first eleven chapters of Genesis: ". . . there should be a careful examination in great detail of the literary tradition of the ancient eastern people, their psychology, their manner of self-expression and *the precise notion which they had of historical truth*."[11] If we are willing to admit that the Israelites excelled other nations in historical consciousness and in storytelling power, we must also admit that they had no knowledge of critical history. Similarly, the Church Fathers cannot solve our problem; for they never faced it. It would be anachronistic to demand an answer from them, except to the extent that they addressed themselves to analogous problems.

Father Vaccari points out still further characteristics of patristic exegesis. The Greek Fathers, he says, were in a situation incomparably superior to ours as far as the understanding of the New Testament is concerned; for they found in it their own language, mentality, institutions, and the like. But,

> With regard to the Old Testament the situation was quite different. The original text was no longer a thing of sound and memory, but rather a translation of vary-

ing quality, which ranged from a slavish copying to a Sybilline obscurity. At other times, it was free even to the point of inaccuracy, or possessed little or no intelligibility, and was almost always clothed in language modeled on a radically different idiom. The people involved in the book lived in a far-distant age and had customs, social institutions, and viewpoints entirely foreign to the Greek mind. The Greek commentators, even though they wished otherwise, were unable to enter into a world so foreign to them, and thus lacked an essential requirement for the proper understanding of the sacred text.[12]

Nevertheless, as Pius XII brings out, the Fathers of the Church kept an open mind and had deep insight into the religious meaning of the Old Testament:

For, although sometimes less instructed in profane learning and in the knowledge of languages than the Scripture scholars of our time, nevertheless, by reason of the office assigned to them by God in the Church, they are distinguished for their subtle insights into heavenly things and for their wonderful sharpness of intellect, which enabled them to penetrate to the very inmost meaning of the Divine Word and to bring to light all that might help to clarify the teaching of Christ and promote holiness of life.[13]

Here is an example of patristic interpretation of the Old Testament. Psalm 87 (Vulgate 86) sings of the glory of Jerusalem, the chosen city of God:

His foundation upon the holy mountains
    the Lord loves:
The gates of Zion,
    more than any dwelling of Jacob.
Glorious things are said of you,
    O city of God!
I tell of Rahab and Babylon
    among those that know the Lord;
Of Philistia, Tyre, Ethiopia:
    "This man was born there."
And of Zion they shall say:
    "One and all were born in her;
And he who has established her
    is the Most High Lord."
They shall note, when the peoples are enrolled:
    "This man was born there."
And all shall sing, in their festive dance:
    "My home is within you."

St. Augustine comments on the name of Rahab which
occurs in the Psalm: ". . . she is that prostitute of Jericho
who received the messengers and sent them away by
another road, who believed in the promise, who feared
God, who was told to hang a red handkerchief outside
of her window, that is, to have the sign of the blood of
Christ in front. There she found salvation and has come
to represent the church of the Gentiles."[14] Augustine
is referring here to the events narrated in the book of
Joshua, where a certain Rahab, because of her special
services, was received along with her family into the

elect community of Israel. In attempting to identify her, Augustine committed an obvious error. In Latin spelling, the Rahab of the book of Joshua and the Rahab of the Psalm appear to be identical, though this is not the case in the original Hebrew. In the "square" letters of the Hebrew script, the difference between the letters *h* and *ḥ* is very slight. In fact, the first students of Hebrew hardly made any distinction at all between them. The phonetic difference is also very slight, for the *h* is softly aspirated, while the *ḥ* has a pronounced laryngeal gasp. This slight difference is all that is required to distinguish two different beings, Rahab and Raḥab. The book of Joshua tells about the first, while the Psalm sings of the second, representing Egypt by this metaphorical name.

Despite this error, there is still some value to Augustine's explanation. Rahab was a Gentile woman who was made a member of God's chosen people. Similarly, Egypt was a Gentile nation which, according to the Psalm, will be accounted among God's faithful. Both cases, therefore, constitute a prelude or announcement of the Church to come, one which is open to all nations. We can see, then, that St. Augustine has grasped the profound religious universalism of the Psalm in spite of the mistake caused by his lack of technical skill.

We could cite many other similar examples, and it is no irreverence to say that the Fathers of the Church are subject to criticism in their interpretation of Scripture. Sometimes they reflect a dogmatic tradition, and are therefore trustworthy. But quite often they bear witness to a cultural tradition which is no longer relevant to the present day. One should not therefore be surprised at the fact that the modern biblical critic handles philological, literary, and historical problems in a way which was not envisioned by the Church Fathers. Pius XII endorses this view in his encyclical: "Let them bear in mind above all that in the rules and laws promulgated by the Church there is question of doctrine regarding faith and morals; but that in the immense matter contained in the Sacred Books—legislative, historical, sapiential, and prophetical—there are very few texts whose sense has been defined by the authority of the Church, nor are there a greater number of texts on which the teaching of the Holy Fathers is unanimous."[15] The pope therefore lays down two restrictions on the authority of the Fathers: first, it is limited to questions of faith or morals; and secondly, even within this narrow category, there is seldom any unanimous consent among the Fathers.

THE CATHOLIC VIEWPOINT:
FIFTY YEARS AGO AND TODAY

Though the viewpoint of the modern biblical scholar is not essentially different from that of the Church

Fathers, it does differ radically from the critical position held by most Catholic scholars fifty years ago. At that time Catholic scholars posed the question of biblical historicity with full awareness of the whole field of modern historical criticism. They knew von Ranke's theory of history and employed it freely. Due to the lack of sufficient data, however, these scholars were unclear in their explanations. The whole question became emotionally charged when the doctrine of scriptural inerrancy was under fire.

The present-day scholar, on the other hand, begins his work in a peaceful atmosphere, where polemic has yielded to abundant evidence and calm judgment. In the words of Scripture, the modern critic has entered upon labors which he did not begin and reaped where he did not sow. Due to this freedom of activity, the interpreters of Scripture have brought forth theories which have shocked some, while they have consoled others. My only hope is that this book will add to the peace which can be derived from a proper understanding of the sacred text.

Many Christians, of course, can read the Bible without ever posing the question of historicity. But those who are searching for a more complete religious training and a better understanding of the Scriptures, must face the critical problems. It would be fruitless for them to seek answers from those who have not followed the development of studies as outlined by Pius XII. They certainly should not consult mere biblical dilettantes who might offer a facile solution without any solid foundation.[16] But when the student of the Bible has recourse to the trained scholar for an answer to his questions, we can only hope that he has not been prejudiced from the start or already scandalized. The scholar's answers will only be understood by one who hears them with an open mind.

The Bible is a divine book written in human words. This literary incarnation of the divine mind has often been likened to the physical incarnation of the Word. Here is an example of such a comparison from a book by Gustav Closen, S.J.:

> The thoughts of God, at least as they exist in God eternally, are by nature divine and purely spiritual. Hence they are completely free from the limits and obscurities which characterize our own human knowledge. Still, God has put down His thoughts in writing for us in the garb of human thought . . .
>
> Through the double incarnation of the Word of God, man has been enabled to cooperate in achieving the union of the divine and the human. This is exemplified by the Virgin Mary in the incarnation of Christ; for she received the Word of God "by the power of the Holy Spirit." In the case of Holy Scripture, the evangelist, apostle, or prophet received the word of God . . . "by the power of the Holy Spirit." For their part, Mary and the biblical writers gave their own flesh and blood. Jesus of Nazareth must therefore have resembled His Mother. Whoever saw them in the

streets of Nazareth must have thought, "There goes a mother with her son." Similarly, the spiritual child engendered by the prophet or evangelist bears a close resemblance to the inspired author. The qualities of the human writer can be deduced from the qualities of his inspired book. Thus the spiritual child is son to both the inspired author and the word of God. In much the same fashion, Mary's child was His Mother's Son, but also the Word of God.[17]

The image of an incarnate God suffering and dying upon a cross seemed foolish to the pagans and scandalous to the Jews. But to the believer, this suffering of the Word of God is a true source of power and virtue. The Bible is also human and seems to suffer. Some have laughed, while others have been scandalized by its problems and limitations, its mysteries and obscurities. But we believe and know that this book contains the power and virtue of God. It is a power arising from words and ready to operate every time we pick up the book in a sincere search for God and His thoughts:

> For just as from the heavens
> the rain and snow come down
> And do not return there
> till they have watered the earth,
> making it fertile and fruitful,
> Giving seed to him who sows
> and bread to him who eats,
> So shall my word be
> that goes forth from my mouth;

It shall not return to me void,
   but shall do my will,
     achieving the end for which I sent it.

Isaiah 55:10–11

The grass withers, the flower wilts,
   when the breath of the Lord blows upon it.
Though the grass withers and the flower wilts,
   the word of our God stands forever.

Isaiah 40:7–8

# Notes

## CHAPTER I

1. Peter Nober, S.J., of the Pontifical Biblical Institute, publishes each year in the periodical *Biblica* a catalogue containing an almost exhaustive list of the books and articles (with notes about book reviews) published all over the world on the subject of the Bible (*Biblica*. Commentarii editi cura Pontificii Instituti Biblici, Roma). This painstaking and highly useful catalogue listed, in 1952, 2,678 titles; in the following year, 3,106; in 1954, 3,027 titles. In 1955 we find a new section, "Conventions, Societies, Institutes" (24 titles). In 1956 we discover another new section, unlabeled, which deals with the dissemination of the Bible and contains 52 titles. The next year another new section appeared with the label, "Practical Hermeneutics, Biblical Movements, etc.," and which contained 88 titles. In 1958 the same section listed 128 titles. In 1960 this section was transferred to the less technical periodical published by the Biblical Institute, *Verbum Domini*, and listed 300 titles. There we find information regarding biblical activity in various countries such as Argentina, Belgium, Brazil, United States, Germany, Switzerland, Italy, Holland, Poland; biblical conventions are mentioned as well as bibliospiritual activity, which refers, for the most part, to meditations; bibliciliturgical activity has 39 titles; there are also categories for biblicocatechetical and pedagogical activity, biblicopastoral activity (especially with regard to preaching), biblicocultural activity, which includes literature, painting, music, and even movies, and phonograph recordings.

2. ["S. Tommaso e Lutero nella storia dell' esegesi," *Civiltà cattolica*, 2 (1935), 561–575; 3 (1935), 36–47. The quoted section is from the latter article, pp. 37–39—Tr.]

3. "Possunt et haec ad beneficia gratiae referri et tunc in his omnia mysteria Christi numerantur" (*Expositio in aliquot libros Veteris Testamenti*, vol. I: *In Psalmos Davidis expositio*).

4. "Judaei ad litteram exponunt de filio Isaiae" (*loc. cit., In Isaiam Prophetam expositio*).

5. "Haec expositio non est tantae auctoritatis sicut superior quae fuit supra VII de alio signo quia magis extorta est et ex Scriptura non habet auctoritatem" (*ibid.*).

6. *Ibid.*, "Non est inconveniens, si hoc intellegatur ad litteram, ita tamen quod puer iste sit figura Christi."

7. "Hunc titulum dignissime fert Christus morte sua qui praedatur infernum. . . . Ita hic Esaiae filius nomen gerit" (*Martin Luthers Werke* [Weimar: Hermann Böhlaus Nachfolger, 1914], vol. 31, II, p. 62).

8. ["In particular, however, we accept the Hebrew text of the Old Testament as derived from the tradition of the Jewish church to whom 'the oracles of God were once entrusted,' and we wish to retain this text today, even down to the vowels and consonants, and either the pointing itself or at least the meaning of the pointing . . ." (H. A. Niemeyer, *Collectio Confessionum in ecclesiis reformatis publicatarum* [Leipzig: J. Klinkhardt, 1840], p. 731). The passage is also cited in Christian Pesch, S.J., *De Inspiratione Sacrae Scripturae* (Herder: Freiburg im Breisgau, 1925), p. 213.

[The following seventeenth-century texts from Protestant writers are also illustrative of this way of thinking:

["We cannot allow the opinion that the Hebrew text of today is written in words different from the ones that came from the hands of Moses and the prophets" (Johann Gerhard, *Loci theologici* (9 vols., 1610–1622), cited in Pesch, *op. cit.*, p. 219).

["The style of the New Testament is free from any blemish due to linguistic blunders and bad grammar" (Johann Andreas Quenstedt, *Theologia didactico-polemica* (1685), cited in Pesch, *op. cit.*, p. 222).—Tr.]

9. H. Rost, in his book on the Bible in the Middle Ages (*Die Bibel im Mittelalter* [Augsburg: M. Seitz, 1939]), lists 817 biblical manuscripts in German, among them twenty-two complete bibles, 342 psalters, and so forth. Previous to the time of Luther (1522), eighteen editions of the Bible were printed in the vernacular in Germany.

10. [*Reden und Aufsätze* (Göttingen: Vandenhoeck & Ruprecht, 1913), pp. 16–17.—Tr.]

11. "La controversia sobre los géneros literarios bíblicos desde fines del siglo pasado hasta nuestros días," *Los géneros literarios de la Sagrada Escritura* (Barcelona: Juan Flors, 1957), pp. 1–40.

12. [See Leopold Fonck, S.J., *Der Kampf um die Wahrheit*

*der H. Schrift seit 25 Jahren* (Innsbruck: Rauch, 1905), pp. 3–14.—Tr.]

13. *Ibid.*, pp. 94–100 (on Fr. Lagrange); pp. 114–121 (on Fr. von Hummelauer). The quotation cited is on p. 5 of Fr. Prado's article, footnote.—Tr.]

14. [See R. T. Murphy, *Père Lagrange and the Scriptures* (Milwaukee: Bruce, 1946).—Tr.]

15. [Lino Murillo, S.J., *Crítica y exegesis: Observaciones sobre un nuevo sistema exegético de la Biblia* (Madrid: Gabriel L. y del Horno, 1905). See especially pp. 68–74. The last quotation cited is on pp. 73 and 74. See also Prado, *art. cit.*, pp. 9–13.—Tr.]

16. [*Journal of Biblical Literature*, 66 (1947), 467–468. The book being reviewed is *A Companion to the Old Testament* by John E. Steinmüller, trans. Kathryn Sullivan, R.S.C.J.—Tr.]

17. [See E. F. Siegman, C.PP.S., "The Decrees of the Pontifical Biblical Commission: A Recent Clarification," *The Catholic Biblical Quarterly*, 18 (1956), 23–29.—Tr.]

18. S. Muñoz Iglesias, *Doctrina pontificia* (Madrid: B.A.C., 1955), No. 76.

19. [*Enchiridion biblicum* (Rome, 1961), Nos. 290, 288, 286, 290.—Tr.]

20. The recent success of Keller's book may be some indication of the attitude toward the Bible in Germany. [Werner Keller, *Und die Bibel hat doch recht* (Düsseldorf: Econ-Verlag, 1956). First published in October, 1955, there were 200,000 volumes in print in August, 1956. In the same year it was translated into English by William Neil under the title, *The Bible As History.*—Tr.]

21. *Art. cit.*, p. 467.

22. *The Faith of Israel* (Philadelphia: Westminster, 1957), pp. 57–59.

23. *Orientalistische Literaturzeitung*, 34 (1931), 852.

24. *Which Books Belong in the Bible?* (Philadelphia: Westminster, 1957), p. 164.

25. [*Divino afflante Spiritu* (from *The Catholic Mind*, 42 [May, 1944], pp. 263, 264, 265, 267, 272 and 273). For the sake of clarity, I have changed a word or phrase here and there from the very literal version cited throughout this book.—Tr.]

26. *Sacra Pagina*, 1 (Gembloux: Éditions J. Duculot, 1959), pp. 15–16.

27. *Divino afflante Spiritu*, pp. 276–277.

CHAPTER II

1. [The "pilpul" was a meticulous method of Talmudic study of the Mosaic Law which sought to explain it and eliminate contradictions by casuistic distinctions, ingenious deductions, and even riddles.—Tr.]

2. The Imagists were Jansenists of the seventeenth century who gave exclusive preference to the parables in Scripture, interpreting them rather arbitrarily.

3. The previously cited *Formula consensus Helvetica* (1675) finally prohibited the use of textual criticism on the Hebrew text (Pesch, *op. cit.*, p. 213): "We cannot in any way approve of the opinion of those persons who maintain that the reading in the Hebrew text is constructed exclusively by human judgment, and who wish to collate the Hebrew reading, which they consider rather poor, from the Septuagint and other Greek translations, from the Samaritan codex, the Aramaic Targums or from any other source. In fact we disapprove of them whenever they have no scruple in emending the text on the basis of reason alone. Further, these men refuse to acknowledge any authentic reading except the one which can be drawn from the exercise of a critical human judgment and employed on variant readings after they have been collated among each other and compared to the Hebrew text itself, a text which they claim has been corrupted in many ways. . . . And thus they bring into question not only the very principle of our faith, but also its sacrosanct authority."

4. [For an excellent treatment of Simon and his work, see Jean Steinmann, *Richard Simon et les origines de l'exégèse biblique* (Paris: Desclée de Brouwer, 1960).—Tr.]

5. The Masoretes were Jewish scholars of the sixth to eighth centuries after Christ who copied and edited the Hebrew Bible and wrote the Masora, i.e., marginal glosses on the text.

6. [*Histoire critique du Vieux Testament* (Rotterdam, 1685). The excerpts cited are drawn from the last 5 pages of the lengthy and, unfortunately, unpaginated preface.—Tr.]

7. [*Disquisitiones biblicae*, vol. I, (2nd ed.; Luca, 1769), 416, 429. These excerpts are from the First Chapter (*Moses revera Pentateuchum scripsit*) of the Fifth Book of the *Disquisitiones.* —Tr.]

8. "Among the Catholics the new historicocritical method was bitterly attacked by J. Bossuet (+1704), who, accustomed as he was to theological speculations, abhorred the rashness of critical methodology. At his instigation, the first book published by R. Simon was condemned and suppressed shortly after its publication, and the author was expelled from the Congregation of the Oratory. . . . It cannot be denied that in the works of R. Simon some conjectures were made which were indeed rash, but, on the other hand, J. Bossuet frequently made unjust and imprudent judgments" (P. Benno Gut, *Introductio Generalis in Sacram Scripturam* [4th ed.; Rome, 1940], p. 9).

9. A. Valbuena Prat, *Historia de la literatura Española* (2nd ed.; Barcelona, 1946), Vol. I, p. 569.

10. *Conjectures sur les mémoires originaux dont il paroit que Moyse s'est servi pour composer le Livre de la Genèse* (Brussels, 1753). [Actually, as the text will make clear, the book was published in Paris. In 1789 it was translated into German.—Tr.]

11. C. W. Ceram, *Gods, Graves and Scholars—The Story of Archaeology*, trans. by E. B. Garside (New York: Knopf, 1952). [But see also J. Finegan, *Light from the Ancient Past* (2nd ed.; Princeton: University Press, 1959).—Tr.]

12. Keller, *op. cit.*, p. x.

13. *Ibid.*, p. 51.

14. *Ibid.*, p. 163.

15. (London, 1912). (Revised ed.; Oberlin, Ohio: Bibliotheca Sacra, 1924).

16. Lachish is a city in South Palestine. The letters were dated at 589/588 B.C.

17. (Philadelphia: Westminster, 1957), pp. 17–18.

18. *Ibid.*, p. 27.

19. *Divino afflante Spiritu*, p. 265.

## CHAPTER III

1. *Divino afflante Spiritu*, pp. 277–278.

2. L. Weisgerber, among others, has developed this point skillfully over the past thirty years. See, e.g., *Von den Kräften der deutschen Sprache*, 4 vols. (2nd. ed.; Düsseldorf, 1958/1959).

3. *Divino afflante Spiritu,* p. 275.

4. J. Prado, C.SS.R., *art. cit. (supra,* Chap. I, n. 11), has related the several incidents which occurred in the fight over literary forms.

5. *Divino afflante Spiritu,* pp. 274–275.

6. *Ibid.,* pp. 275–276.

7. [See *Das Buch Esther* (Bonn: Peter Hansten, 1948), pp. 23–33.—Tr.]

8. [*The Catholic Mind* (November, 1950), p. 699. The letter referred to in the first sentence of the quotation was written by the Pontifical Biblical Commission in January, 1948 to Cardinal Suhard, then archbishop of Paris. It dealt with the date of the sources of the Pentateuch and the literary type of the first eleven chapters of Genesis.—Tr.]

9. *Biblica* 6 (1925), 250.

10. This point is also made in *Divino afflante Spiritu* (p. 272): "For not a few things, especially in matters pertaining to history, were scarcely at all or not fully explained by the commentators of past ages, since they lacked almost all the information which was needed for their clearer exposition."

11. *Enchiridion biblicum,* 1961 (3rd ed.), No. 581. It would be illegitimate to misinterpret the underlined words, contrary to the intention of the author and contrary to the moderate expression employed. I think that my distinction clears up the meaning of the statement to some degree.

12. *Art. cit.,* pp. 252–253.

13. *Divino afflante Spiritu,* pp. 271–272.

14. *Enarratio in Psalmos,* 86, 4 (PL 37, 1105–1106).

15. *Divino afflante Spiritu,* p. 278.

16. It is illuminating in this connection to read a few passages from the address delivered by Bishop Charue of Namur at the Louvain Biblical Congress (*Sacra Pagina,* I, pp. 78, 79, 85):

"No one can deny that the Church relies on theologians for a better understanding and a proper presentation of revealed truth, or that she is grateful to them for rendering the service of an invaluable cooperation with the heirarchy. Now among the theologians, the exegetes have a special mission, namely to read, to interpret, to evaluate clearly, and finally to present the books of Sacred Scripture to the Christian people in a manner which is accurate, appropriate, and edifying. It seems to me that it is both urgent and necessary in the current biblical movement to acknowledge the special task which the exegetes have to treat of biblical matters under the vigilance and ultimate responsibility of the hierarchy and to be, ever since the biblical movement began, the accredited guides for all those whose duty it is to make the bread of Scripture available to souls.

"Catholic exegetes are aware of the importance and delicate nature of this task. We know that they are applying themselves to it wholeheartedly, with devotion, and even with enthusiasm, and we believe they are responding very well, in general, to the confidence which the Church has placed in them. Are they mistaken at times? Do they sometimes become upset or even quit their labors temporarily because of certain decisions made by religious authorities? Must we believe that those who never make mistakes would always for that reason be more cooperative with the hierarchy? The Biblical Commission recognizes the fact that these interruptions do not always put an end to the study of the problems under discussion, and that the scholars can apply themselves faithfully to their scientific labors, provided they are disposed to submit themselves to the judgment of the Church, the guardian of Sacred Scripture. In fact, it is precisely the Catholic biblical scholars who recognize so well the fact that they should be attentive to all the voices of tradition, to the teaching authority of the Church, to those who brought light on the subject in centuries gone by, and especially to those who perform this function today. Their only desire is to be sons who are submissive to the Church in their exegetical studies and in their biblical apostolate.

"But the exegetes are also aware that the treasure contained in the holy books can only be made available as a result of persistent and methodical labor, and that this labor, along with the prayer which accompanies it, is indeed necessary to the exercise of the teaching mission entrusted by Christ to His Church. These scholars offer to the hierarchy their good will, their labors, and the results of their studies. And we can also say that the hierarchy, on its part, awaits this cooperation with confidence and accepts it with gratitude. The Holy See has seen fit, therefore, to publish important biblical encyclicals, to found the Biblical Institute of Rome, and to encourage many other projects directed toward the scientific study of Holy Scripture. Furthermore, many decisions of both Pius XI and Pius XII lean in the direction of reserving the courses of Scripture taught in the universities, seminaries, and scholasticates to those who possess an academic degree from the Biblical

Commission or the Pontifical Biblical Institute. This insistence on the part of Rome strengthens us in our conviction that, save for exceptional and therefore rare cases, the use of the Bible cannot be understood in the Church without the cooperation of professional exegetes, men who are well prepared for this task by serious study. . . .

"My own opinion is that the Church has every intention of thus reserving for its biblical scholars a virtual monopoly within their own competence, provided that it is exercised in proper cooperation with the hierarchy. Such men cannot be arbitrarily substituted for by teachers who are not approved for the task by the Church or simply by men of zealous activity, men of efficiency, as the saying goes, but men who are not always familiar with the problems of scriptural interpretation."

17. *Wege in Die Heilige Schrift* (Regensburg: Friedrich Pustet, 1955), pp. 13–14.